OBSERVATIONS

For Young Architects

OBSERVATIONS

For Young Architects

CESAR PELLI

THE MONACELLI PRESS

To Diana Balmori,
   my most important collaborator

First published in the United States of America
in 1999 by
The Monacelli Press, Inc.
10 East 92nd Street, New York, New York 10128.

Copyright © 1999 The Monacelli Press, Inc.

Library of Congress Cataloging-in-Publication Data
Pelli, Cesar.
Observations for young architects / Cesar Pelli.
p. cm.
ISBN 1-58093-031-X
1. Architecture—Philosophy. I. Title.
NA2500.P435   1999
720'.1—dc21   98-52134

Printed and bound in Singapore

Designed by Abigail Sturges

CONTENTS

ACKNOWLEDGMENTS

I first lectured on architecture and its connections at the University of Illinois in 1977. I have expanded on this and other ideas included here in further lectures and in interviews and magazine articles. In giving form to this book, I was greatly aided by the suggestions of Victoria Solan, my research assistant, and of Denis and Rafael Pelli, my sons and toughest critics. I am very grateful to my secretary, Carolann Morrissey, for her advice and for typing and retyping my innumerable revisions, and to Janet Kagan, our former director of communications, and Justin Shigemi, her assistant, for their help in locating images and obtaining photography rights. I am also indebted to my teachers, clients, associates, and collaborators for their thoughts and examples, which, through the years, have helped me develop and refine the observations described in these pages.

INTRODUCTION

I have been immersed in architecture since my adolescence. The more I practice architecture, the more varied and rewarding I find it. Every project presents me with new worlds to know and respond to. As I continue to learn about my profession, my understanding of its richness and complexity deepens and so does my admiration for those who practice it well. In this book, I would like to share with those interested in architecture my observations of many years.

The art of architecture

Architecture is one of the great arts. We find proof of this in the depth of emotion that good buildings provoke in us. These emotions are comparable (and for me, superior) to those provoked by good paintings and sculptures. Buildings such as Hagia Sophia, Katsura Palace, and Notre Dame du Haut at Ronchamp are sublime artistic achievements. They validate our art in the same way that Shakespeare's *King Lear,* Bach's *Saint Matthew Passion,* and Rembrandt's *Night Watch* validate the arts of theater, music, and painting.

The practice of an art is an end in itself. We work toward a necessary result, perhaps a sublime result, but the creative act is in the practice.

Sometimes the product is evanescent, as in music or dance, and sometimes it is an object, which can be considered the art's residue, and which may be bought and sold. But we cannot buy or sell the creative act. It remains ours alone. I am concerned with all aspects of architectural practice, but this book is written primarily for those who see architecture as an art.

When a building I have designed is finally finished, I experience two strong but conflicting feelings. I am filled with satisfaction in the accomplishment, and feel the incomparable pleasure of seeing the building for the first time, complete in the weather and the world, being used and enjoyed. At the same time, the pleasure is accompanied by a sense of loss, of knowing that my creative labors on the project are now over. This moment of separation comes in all artistic pursuits but it is particularly acute in architecture. Painters, poets, and composers can keep revising their work until they can take it no further, but for architects the completion of a building is final. In that first moment in which we see our work in its totality, it is no longer ours to affect.

Pondering our art, we may ask ourselves, "What makes a good building?" and "What is good architecture?" We then find that answering these questions is as difficult as answering, "What makes a good person?" or "What is a good life?" These are complex and important issues that cannot be reduced to a single quality. Sometimes we feel that one aspect of a building (perhaps its beauty) is so extraordinary that all flaws can be forgiven. We do this with people too. But these judgments apply only to the public faces of people or architecture. They are sufficient if we see them only in movies or as tourists. We need more if we have to live with them. We can get closer to the real worth of a building or a person if we consider their various qualities, weighing each differently, depending on the circumstances.

In trying to understand our art we may keep in mind that not only buildings that flaunt their aesthetic intentions are artistically valuable; so are many modest structures that have been designed with love and care. We may also keep in mind that art is not a quality that exists in the thing itself. It is a value we assign to objects or activities based on the reactions they provoke in us. The touchstone I use to consider any building art is that somehow, to some degree, it must move me. I may be influenced by the opinions of others, but I see as art only what reaches and touches me. What society sees as art depends on a forever shifting consensus formed by a multitude of opinions from everywhere, weighted by influence.

Legitimacy

Architecture is a profession as well as an art. These are not separate activities but two aspects of a single experience. Society, however, classifies professionals and artists into separate categories and measures them with different yardsticks. The relative worth of these two aspects of architecture varies with cultures and times. Both the profession and the art of architecture require legitimacy. Throughout most of human history, legitimacy was conferred by church or state. Important religious and civic buildings were legitimate, and therefore were valued as architecture, even before the architect was engaged. The building could be bad architecture, but it was still architecture. Practically all other buildings were not architecture, no matter how beautiful, necessary, or appropriate they were. What we would call today the artistic value of a building did not affect its legitimacy or its status. State and church no longer have such authority. An architecture for our time requires a new legitimacy. In this book, I will touch on some arguments made for the legitimacy of modern architecture. These arguments are important because they define our shared ideals.

Rules and beliefs

To be considered good architecture, our work must conform to a complex set of rules, consisting of accepted theories, formal models, and ideals. The contemporary rules for designing and judging architecture put such a premium on original talent that only a handful of architects have been able to master them. Examples from the past demonstrate that when rules and expectations are reasonable, most architects can design good buildings. Any society should expect that architects' rules will produce good buildings most of the time. This is what a healthy architecture does. The evidence of the majority of our buildings suggests that there is something wrong with today's rules. They do not suit our cities and need to be reconsidered. This book is my contribution toward that end.

The final result of our work is making cities. It is our greatest responsibility. If we do not make beautiful, enjoyable, and workable cities, we are not going to be worth much in that history that we all prize, no matter how brilliant our individual efforts may be.

I am not writing about specific buildings, architects, or styles, but about the nature of our art—the beliefs that shape us, our buildings, and our cities. Many books and articles have been written on architectural theories. Here I will advance no new design theory but propose that an understanding of the principal factors affecting architecture is necessary for an intelligent practice. To achieve a global overview—and because I write not as a scholar but as a practicing architect—I will present historical developments in a very simplified form. At the end of each chapter, I will amplify my general observations with concrete examples from my personal experience. These may also help to reveal the origins of my thoughts. I hope my story will interest anyone who loves architecture, but I am writing mainly with students and young architects in mind. I hope they will find my observations helpful as they start to give form to their most important design, that of their practice and career.

OBSERVATIONS

For Young Architects

CONNECTIONS

The light dove clearing in free flight the thin air, whose resistance it feels, might imagine that her movements would be far more free and rapid in airless space.

—Immanuel Kant, 1781

When we design, our hands are tugged in many directions by architecture's connections with the world. These connections limit and strengthen our art, but are seldom well understood. Too many architects seem to spend their energies resisting the consequences of these connections instead of harnessing their forces to advance the design. Freedom of action in architecture is an illusion that can keep us from gaining control of our craft and enjoying the practice of our art.

Eight connections

Observing architecture through its connections provides a structure for discussing this complex subject and also reveals views of our art. Architecture's many connections with reality vary in importance, and, depending on the times, some raise more issues than others. I have chosen eight principal connections on which to base my observations. They seem to give the most complete view of architecture and form the most coherent groupings. But the number is arbitrary. Someone else might choose different groupings and end up with more or fewer connections, seeing other things through them.

The eight connections through which I have chosen to view architecture are:

Time: when a building is built. I propose we take another look at the definitions of *our time* and *modern architecture* (the architecture of our time) because they affect what is considered acceptable in our art.

Construction: how buildings are built. An architecture grows only when it is rooted in a living tradition of construction. *Frame and enclosure*, our dominant system of construction, is still new and developing.

Place: where a building is built. The place is the whole; the new building will be a part of this whole. This implies a responsibility that often conflicts with other cherished goals of architects.

Purpose: why a building is built. A building is a shelter for human activities and a physical expression of human aspirations. The purpose of a building often defines the public character of its architecture.

Culture: what shapes our minds. *Architectural culture*, through our education, apprenticeship, and practice, affects us for life. The *art world* also affects us; in this century, for example, painting has profoundly influenced our view of ourselves.

Design process: how we design—our craft. Contemporary practice is complex, based on teamwork, and itself requires design.

Constituency: for whom we design. Those who select the architect, pay the bills, use the building, and judge its success have a formidable effect on our designs and careers.

Oneself: how we shape ourselves. Through our lives, we develop a body of ideas and principles that guides our actions.

Connections impose limits that are encountered by every architect. These limits are always addressed in one way or another, but that is not enough. A mishandled connection can abort the project, weaken the architecture, or damage a place.

In centuries past, understanding our connectedness was a natural and inevitable part of architectural practice, which was learned by doing under the guidance of an experienced architect, in the studio and at the construction site. Now it is learned in school, a more abstract and detached system, with interests and goals of its own. Because schools are removed from practice, we must make a special effort to understand the connections that sustain architecture.

Disconnections

It is possible to ignore some connections, but doing so undermines the architecture. Ranch-style houses are built on flat pads cut into hills, doing violence to their *place*. Tudor and Spanish Colonial houses are built today, denying their own *time*. Lightweight walls are designed to look as if they were solid and load-bearing, falsifying their *construction*. Buildings disconnected from their physical and cultural environment are built every day. Architects can downplay some connections in the design of individual buildings, but no healthy architecture can develop based on sustained disconnections with reality.

Historic changes in architecture resulted from efforts to correct the cumulative effect of disregarded connections. Such strivings gave birth to modern architecture. Starting in the mid-nineteenth century, many architects working far apart and using diverse formal systems sought a new architecture to replace the then dominant classical style, although it had produced many great buildings and cities. This ancient system of design had failed to adapt to new realities and many felt that architecture could not endure as a living art so disconnected.

It is telling that the very connections that were troubling for classicism became central themes in the ideology of the new architecture. The classical style seemed unresponsive to the new functions of a changed society, and the modern reaction gave function a key role in the design process. The classical style seemed disconnected from industrial construction technology, and the modern reaction led to structural expression and a preference for industrial materials. Of course, modernists also had other motivations, but reconnection was at the root of their attempts to create a new architecture.

Much of the richness of architecture, as buildings and as practice, derives from its multiple connections with life. Understanding them, in the forms they take in a particular time and a particular place, is a necessary step in comprehending the art to which we have dedicated ourselves.

My appreciation for the connectedness of architecture did not begin during my school years but afterward, as I started participating in its practice. It was then that I saw how carrying an intention from design to building, and the very power of buildings, are dependent on the intelligent understanding of the limits and potentials of their connections. I also began to notice that the relative importance of different connections to a design varies according to the characteristics of each project.

After my apprenticeship with Eero Saarinen, I became director of design at DMJM (Daniel, Mann, Johnson, and Mendenhall) in Los Angeles in 1964. This was a critical moment for me because I was testing my wings and trying to understand the air currents. Anthony Lumsden had agreed to come with me from the Saarinen office to DMJM as assistant director of design, and our first design there was part of a planning project in the Santa Ynez Valley in the Santa Monica Mountains of Los Angeles called Sunset Mountain Park. Sunset International Petroleum, the client, had come to DMJM's planning department with a request for a master plan for single-family houses, each one on its own lot. The site was quite steep and riddled with faults, and the rather conventional plan developed after some two years of work proved to be physically and financially impractical. The review committee, which included Pietro Belluschi, George Dudley, Carl Feiss, A. Q. Jones, and Peter Walker, suggested that I be brought in to take a fresh look at the problem.

I was new to the project and thought that the answer could come from the qualities of the extraordinary site. There was a rocky knob, like a promontory, toward one end of the bowl-shaped valley, which seemed to suggest a solution, and Lumsden and I proposed building there a dense complex of 1,500 dwellings with a "town center" that we labeled the Urban Nucleus (fig. 1). The structure was to be built "hugging" the rock, following the contours of the terrain to become one with the site. The concentration of much of the housing on the knob left a large area of the site free for parks. This proposal, although unconventional, was the only one that the client's technical advisers thought capable of answering the geological and economic requirements of the project. In the end, Sunset Oil ran into financial difficulties in other real-estate investments, the project was abandoned, and the site for the Urban

Nucleus was sold to become part of a state park. That knob in the Santa Monica Mountains is the most charged natural site on which I have ever worked. The intimate connection of our design with its place gave it logic and strength.

Two years later, in 1967, we designed another housing project, but for different circumstances. DMJM was asked by a Hawaiian developer, Clarence Ching, to design an 822-unit neighborhood of public housing in Honolulu, Kukui Gardens. Ching was competing with two other development teams for this project. The climate of Hawaii was a significant factor, but the twenty-acre site was flat and indifferent. Most important for us was the nature of public housing, the purpose of the

1. Cesar Pelli and Anthony Lumsden at DMJM, Sunset Mountain Park: Urban Nucleus, Los Angeles, California, 1965. Model of unbuilt project

2. Cesar Pelli and
Anthony Lumsden
at DMJM, Kukui
Gardens, Honolulu,
Hawaii, 1969

*project. Kukui Gardens was designed to look not like public housing but
like a stable and pleasant neighborhood. We chose the most economical
building module and construction system in order to give the users the
maximum amount of space for the monies available. Taking advantage
of the temperate climate, we gave each unit either a courtyard or a
lanai, which in Hawaii can function almost as an extra room. The
DMJM project was built in 1969 (fig. 2).*

*The project was part of a federal program (221d3) that mandated
that the units be rental only and that when people's salaries increased
beyond certain limits they had to leave the project. These two require-*

ments conspired against any sense of neighborhood stability or communal pride. Even with these negative institutional odds, Kukui Gardens has been very successful and remains sought-after housing.

Sunset Mountain Park and Kukui Gardens were both large-scale residential projects. Our designs for them, however, were quite different because their individual characteristics called for different responses. The design of the first was driven by the nature of its unique place; the design of the second by its social purpose. Throughout this book I describe how, in other projects, I have tried to respond with my designs to the different relative importance of other connections.

TIME

Time and architecture have always been linked in many essential ways. But today, this connection has a special importance because it defines our architecture. In this chapter I will concentrate on two crucial but elusive concepts: one is *our time* and the other is *modern architecture*. These two concepts have had and continue to have a fundamental effect on our thoughts and our buildings. One follows the other because *modern architecture* is the architecture of *our time*. Rarely will an architectural magazine appear without a reference to "our time," "our condition," or "our epoch."

Our time

For architects, *our time* can mean two different things. One is the time period in which each one of us lives, the particular events and ideas that shape our view of the world and art. This is an unavoidable connection in any art and for every artist.

The second meaning of *our time* affects our shared understanding of architecture. *Our time* is defined by new social, technological, and intellectual conditions that created a major break with our past some generations ago. These conditions were considered so unlike those existing before the break that a new architecture was required. It is also apparent that we have not recently experienced any changes of similar magnitude that have made us reconsider again the nature of architecture. The break remains a unique occurrence. Its specific characteristics, when it took place, and what was the most suitable architectural response continue to be matters of debate.

The ideology of international modernism took shape shortly after World War I and reflected the world views of Western European intellectuals. Since that time, the international order has been shaken by World War II and its aftermath. Europe lost its cultural hegemony, colonial empires have been dismantled, and Asia has risen to compete with the West on all fronts. Humanity experienced the Holocaust and the ascent and subsequent failure of totalitarian systems. Atom bombs have been exploded, humans have walked on the moon, societies have made significant advances in civil rights, and much of the world's ecology has been disturbed. Lives have been changed by major scientific developments, such as those in physics and medicine, and new technologies, such as television and computers. This suggests that the phenomenon that is so important to modern architecture cannot be the zeitgeist, the spirit of the time, because that spirit has suffered many violent changes since World War I. For architects, however, our shared understanding of *our time* describes social and technological conditions that have remained constant enough to continue shaping our art. We need to look beyond the zeitgeist and further back than 1919 to find the beginnings of the period that defines *our time*.

Specific events affect the various segments of our culture differently. An art is compelled to change only when there is a direct link between the nature of the change and the nature of the art. The social and political revolutions of the late eighteenth century changed the social role of most artists and the meaning of their work. The industrial revolution affected architecture directly, because advances in engineering and manufacturing gave birth to a new technology of construction. The new social structures had a lasting effect on architecture. Clients and audiences for architects changed, as did the purposes of the buildings being designed. The accumulation of major changes in a rather short period of time defined a new time, *our time*. The characteristics of this new time were already recognized, and gave birth to a new architecture, by the mid-nineteenth century.

Modern architecture

Most architects probably consider modern architecture an extremely important development that affects the direction of their work. Yet the shared understanding of that architecture's historical outline, goals, and main participants remains unfocused and riddled with contradictions. In order to have a clearer idea of this phenomenon, it is necessary to start by considering the word *modern*. This word is vital to architectural discourse, but its meaning changes according to context. The historians' definition of the era that began either in 1453 with the fall of Constantinople or in 1492 with the discovery of America does not help us. The diverse glints of modernity in the arts in the eighteenth century are important as antecedents but not substantial enough to define our subject. We may start with the dictionary's definition of *modern*—"qualifying actions or things as being new, belonging to the present"—because it is at the heart of what matters to us. The term "modern architecture" is applied to at least three distinct but overlapping historical periods, each with quite different implications for our designs.

Modern art

The first use of the term "modern architecture" defines it as an offshoot of the modern movement in art, which may have been born in 1863 at the Salon des Refusés in Paris or, if we follow the influential libretto of the Museum of Modern Art, in the 1880s with Cézanne's paintings of bathers. In this version, modern architecture is part of an artistic revolution led by painting. The influence of painting on architecture was certainly quite strong by the 1920s, but I will argue that the record of modernism in architecture is older and that the Crystal Palace of 1851 (discussed later) is proof of architecture's independence and precedence. This art-influenced view of modern architecture comes from outside architecture. It is embraced by many art critics and museums because it elevates aesthetics as the primary hallmark of modernity. For those who see all the visual arts as one movement, guided by painting, and are concerned only with the formal aspects of architecture, this is a comfortable definition that has gained for architecture a minor gallery in some museums of "art." However, this interpretation does not correspond to the historical data and has created much confusion around architecture.

3. Pablo Picasso,
L'aficionado, *1912*

International modernism

The second use of the term "modern architecture" incorporates many aspects of the first definition, but it mainly refers to a coherent set of architectural ideas and forms developed in Western Europe in the early 1920s. In this view, the break with the past that defines our time was first perceived in its full clarity just after World War I; the successful response was the architecture prescribed by Le Corbusier, the Bauhaus, the Congrès Internationaux d'Architecture Moderne (CIAM), and their followers. Their definition of modernism, and their preferred architectural forms, are, for many, still as valid today as they were in the 1920s. That decade saw the formative and the most creative period of this new architecture. By the 1930s, the formative period was essentially over and ripe for codification. This took place with the Museum of Modern Art's 1932 "Modern Archi-

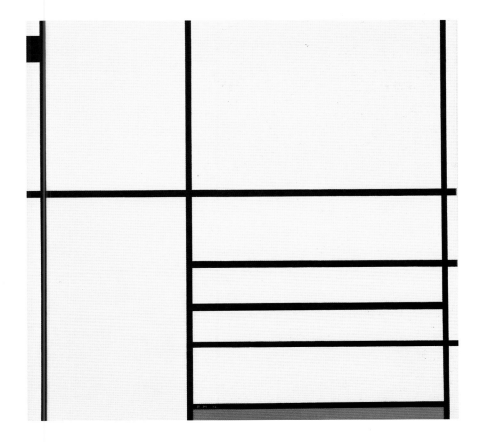

4. *Piet Mondrian,* Composition in white, black and red, *1936*

tecture—International Exhibition" and its book-catalog, which transformed the movement into a style: the International Style. In this combined form it conquered the world of architecture. It has been called international modernism.

By the time international modernism in architecture appeared on the world scene, painting had already reinvented itself with great vigor, becoming the dominant art form. The impact of cubism on the visual arts was so great that it came to be seen as not just a new way of painting but as a major discovery, comparable to the technological and scientific discoveries that changed society's vision of the world. Parallel to cubism, or provoked by it, other artistic efforts flourished; the most important development for architecture was abstract painting. Cubism and abstraction became the new way to see and to design (figs. 3, 4).

Such forms are still apparent in the buildings of many notable architects working today.

In its early years, international modernism had to grow up in the shadow of academic classicism, the first global architectural style, which was still very strong in the 1920s and 1930s. Academic classicism was a comprehensive and effective way to design handsome buildings following the rules taught by the Ecole des Beaux-Arts in Paris. We should note that these rules were based on a vision of society that did not include most of the social and technological changes that took place in the eighteenth and nineteenth centuries. The Ecole opened in 1819. It was most respected and influential in the late nineteenth century and its curriculum remained unchanged until 1968. By the 1920s, it was devitalized, but it was still the predominant architectural style of the major buildings in the developed world. It was also the style used by most prominent architects of the time. Academic classicism was seen by modernists as a major obstacle to the acceptance of their vision. The League of Nations' competition—one of the key events in the life of international modernism—was considered a tragedy for architecture, because the first prize was taken away from Le Corbusier (fig. 5) and an academic design was selected for construction. Anti-classicism has continued to be an important component of this definition of an architecture of our time.

Inclusive modernism

The third, and for me the most accurate and useful, view of modern architecture, refers to the whole of modernity in architecture as shaped by the work of those architects who sensed that irreversible changes were taking place in the world, requiring a new, or *modern*, architecture. These architects were the first to perceive the main characteristics and newness of our time—a time that is still with us, a new time that called for new responses. Some of the early responses were radical, others were evolutionary, and they began in the mid-nineteenth century.

The caliber of international modernism's best architects, the power of its best buildings, and the influence of its teaching were so impressive that many architects came to believe that this movement was the whole of modern architecture and that the earlier efforts were incomplete or imma-

5. Le Corbusier, League of Nations, Geneva, Switzerland, 1927. Competition entry

ture. Nikolaus Pevsner, in his widely read book *Pioneers of the Modern Movement* (1936), retold the story that modern architects working before 1914 were only preparing the ground for the real modernism that came after World War I. His bias was reasonable because he was writing at a time when international modernism was still young and exciting and promised a wonderful new world.

At the turn of the twenty-first century, with the fireworks of the 1920s well in the past, we can look beyond the lights and the smoke at the larger scene, and we can see not only the outstanding architects within international modernism but also the many good architects who were already modern before international modernism appeared on the scene. We need only look at the designs of the "pioneers" to see that they were already true and capable modern architects. I propose Joseph Paxton in England; Charles Rennie Mackintosh in Scotland; Henri Labrouste, Hector Guimard, Tony Garnier, and Auguste Perret in France; Peter Behrens and Hans Poelzig in Germany; H. P. Berlage and Michel de Klerk in Holland; Henry van de Velde and Victor Horta in Belgium; Otto Wagner, Josef Hoffman, Josef Maria Olbrich, and Adolf Loos in Austria; Antonio Sant'Elia in Italy; Antoni Gaudí in Catalonia; and, in the United States, Irving Gill in California; Louis Sullivan and John Wellborn Root in Chicago; and, most important, Frank Lloyd Wright. Wright was one of the best architects of all time, unquestionably modern and yet outside international modernism in time and style. These architects produced great modern works, buildings of our time. They do not anticipate anything but are complete in themselves, and they are still admired and address still-current preoccupations. The reading hall of the Bibliothèque Nationale (Paris, 1868), the Galerie des Machines (Paris, 1889), the Monadnock Building (Chicago, 1892), the Maison du Peuple (Brussels, 1899), the National Farmer's Bank (Owatonna, Minnesota, 1908), the Glasgow School of Art (1909), the AEG Turbine Factory (Berlin, 1909), the Helsinki Railroad Station (1911), the Larkin Building (Buffalo, 1906), and the Robie House (Chicago, 1909) are part of our memories of modernism and continue to

6. Henri Labrouste,
Bibliothèque Nationale,
Paris, France, 1868.
Reading hall

7. *Dutert and Contamin, Galerie des Machines, Paris International Exhibition, 1889. Demolished 1910*

inspire us with their forms (figs. 6-15). All were designed before 1914, and all are evidence of the importance and modernity of their architects' visions. Modernism as a whole was inclusive and exploratory. Its models and its range are well suited to the needs of our cities.

Even after 1920, there were important modern architects who, with all or part of their work, did not quite fit into the prescribed formal canons of international modernism. These architects have usually been claimed as members of the movement to maintain its appearance of universality.

Opposite
8. Burnham and Root,
Monadnock Building,
Chicago, Illinois, 1892

9. Victor Horta, Maison
du Peuple, Brussels,
Belgium, 1899.
Demolished 1965

10. Louis Sullivan,
National Farmer's
Bank, Owatonna,
Minnesota, 1908

Among them are Hans Scharoun, Erich Mendelsohn, Erik Gunnar Asplund, Ivan Leonidov, Raymond Hood, and Eliel Saarinen. Even some buildings by Alvar Aalto, Louis Kahn, and Eero Saarinen refuse to fit comfortably within international modernism.

I am not suggesting that all architectural expressions of modernity were equally developed or are equally in tune with today's sensibilities. This is obviously not the case. Aesthetic results depend on the talent and opportunities of their producers. And our aesthetic judgment is affected by the fashions of the day. My point is that the works of international modernists are not more legitimate than those of Paxton, de Klerk, Sullivan, or

11. Charles Rennie Mackintosh, Glasgow School of Art, Glasgow, Scotland, 1909

12. Peter Behrens,
AEG Turbine Factory,
Berlin, Germany, 1909

Wright. They all are legitimately modern and equally valid as references for our designs and as support for our theories today.

We may conclude that in the most useful and accurate use of the terms, *our time* denotes conditions that began taking form some two centuries ago and *modern architecture* describes the present nature of architecture as it started taking shape in the mid-nineteenth century. This is not to deny international modernism its value. It is modernism's most exciting and important branch. It is a key aspect, but not the whole thing.

The record of great buildings contains evidence that since the mid-nineteenth century, modern architects have been consciously searching for a new architecture, suited to our time and independent of historical styles. This still ongoing search is for an architecture that will be as appropriate to our technology and our social structures as the architectures of ancient Greece and the Middle Ages were to theirs. There are major differences, however: Greek and Gothic architectures were formal systems shaped by religious intentions. They responded to very circumscribed

13. *Eliel Saarinen,*
Railroad Station,
Helsinki, Finland, 1911

building purposes, technologies, and geography with well-developed vocabularies. Modern architecture is not a formal system but an attitude toward design based on loosely shared ideals and beliefs. It embraces all building purposes, a variety of technologies, and many stylistic approaches. It has no religious affiliations and is practiced in all parts of the world.

14. *Frank Lloyd Wright,*
Larkin Building,
Buffalo, New York,
1906. Demolished 1950

15. *Frank Lloyd Wright,*
Robie House, Chicago,
Illinois, 1909

The Crystal Palace

In trying to discern the life span of modern architecture, it becomes desirable to search for its beginnings. Origins of cultural changes are seldom clear, but one way to establish a birth date for an artistic current is to find the earliest critical work that fully expresses its main characteristics. My test relies on the quality of the art produced. The first step is to identify the first complete work of generally accepted excellence: a masterpiece. The second step is to ascertain that the work differed in form and substance from earlier or contemporary work. The third step is to confirm that the aspects in which the work differed from those of its time are part of a new definition of the art, and are still valid today.

Joseph Paxton's Crystal Palace fulfills the conditions of my test and suggests that modern architecture came to life in 1851. Attempts at a new architecture were made in the English and French greenhouses and markets of the 1830s and in some roof structures, such as those of the Galerie d'Orleans (1831) and the Bibliothèque Sainte-Geneviève (1850), but the Crystal Palace is modernism's first entire masterpiece. Erected in 1851 and dismantled in 1852, it was perhaps the most influential modern building created and still has much to teach us.

The importance of the Crystal Palace in modern architecture has not been properly recognized. The building, and the process that made it happen, had qualities of our time—modern qualities that require a careful review. It was built for the Great Exhibition of the Work of All Nations. That the building instantly elicited the popular nickname "the Crystal Palace" tells us that the people of London saw the building as belonging to them.

The Great Exhibition was the first international exhibition intended as a public celebration of the connectedness of the industrialized world. The products to be exhibited, and the public that was expected to come, needed protection from rain, cold, and thieves. This shelter needed to be built in a very short time, to be taken down after a few months, and to cost as little as possible. The erection of a work of architecture was not a stated objective, although it would be, obviously, a desirable by-product. The procedures leading to the selection of a design and a designer have, for us today, a familiarly messy quality. After many confrontations, a site was chosen in Hyde Park and architects from all over the world were invited to submit designs. Two hundred forty-five entries were received, but no first prize was awarded, although two were given special mention. These were the entries by Hector Horeau of Paris and Richard Turner of Dublin. One of the two would have been built, if it had appeared possible to build it with the available time and money. The Building Committee (of the Royal Commission for the Exhibition) then produced its own design, which tried to incorporate the most desirable features of the two best competition entries. That scheme, although lower in estimated cost than those of Turner or Horeau, was still too expensive.

At this point, Joseph Paxton entered the scene. He proposed a design to the Building Committee that, he claimed, would accommodate the needs of the Great Exhibition and could be built within the budget and time available. The Building Committee, still trying to salvage its own design, was not very receptive to Paxton's proposal. In a modern gesture, Paxton then took his scheme directly to the public by publishing it in the *Illustrated London News* on July 6, 1850. Public reaction was very favorable, which forced the Building Committee to reconsider Paxton's scheme. Paxton brought his design again to the Royal Commission, together with a firm bid for construction (by Fox and Henderson) for £79,800—less than the £80,000 the Royal Commission had raised. Fox and Henderson also tendered a firm bid of £141,000 for the construction of the Building Committee's scheme. The bid in both cases was only for the use of the building. The structure, after dismantling, would remain the property of Fox and Henderson.

Paxton was not trained as an architect. He was a gardener, with experience in building greenhouses. This is an important fact, first, because it reminds us that when structures need to be built within constraints, if the architectural profession is not ready to design them successfully, somebody else will. As a profession we cannot drift too far from the realities of the world in which we function, or we will be sidestepped and left behind. Second, because Paxton was free of the preconceptions of the architectural culture, he was able to look realistically at the possibilities of building in our time.

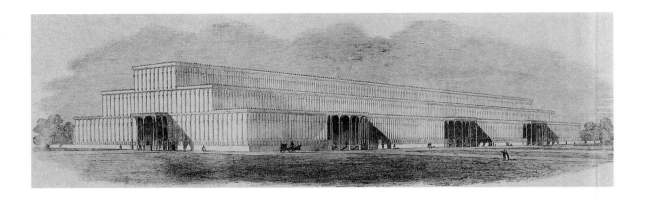

16. *Joseph Paxton,*
Crystal Palace, London,
England, 1851.
Early proposal

Paxton's directness of purpose is best seen in his original scheme: an uninterrupted three-tiered glass extrusion 1,780 feet long (fig. 16). The Building Committee accepted the proposal but requested that a vaulted transept be added to save some large elm trees. The trees were indeed there, but I believe the main urge of the Building Committee was to make the building more "noble," more "architectural." Paxton accommodated the request (fig. 17). This willingness to incorporate the intentions of others in his design, and to turn these impositions into opportunities to make a better building, are qualities that I greatly respect.

Pragmatism guided the design of the structure. Materials were chosen not for their theoretical clarity but because they would do the best job for the lowest cost. Thus cast and wrought iron were used for speed of fabrication and strength, but an ample amount of wood was also used. In fact, there was more wood than iron in the Crystal Palace. This building was not a lesson in advanced technology; rather, it shows the wisdom of making the best use of all available technologies.

As early as 1851, the most suitable construction technology could be one based on manufactured, standardized components. However, at that time this technology made sense only in special circumstances. Masonry construction was still very much alive. Paxton's clarity of mind allowed him to realize that art could be made with a new industrial technology, without exalted historical precedents. He understood that by enclosing space with a material such as glass, rich in perceptual qualities, and using repetitive, industrially produced elements on a vast scale, his design could be extended or reduced, without altering the essential architectural qualities of the building. This was a modern view, the antithesis of the classic Renaissance ideal.

The design proceeded in a very modern way. Paxton produced some simple drawings. Charles Fox designed the details, including the decorative details of the cast-iron pieces, and prepared the working drawings. Owen Jones developed the ornamental refinements, the color scheme (the structure was polychrome), and the painted decorations. Paxton understood the strength of his design and could incorporate the work of others without fear that his vision would be undone.

Paxton's conception was based on practical experience, not academic theory. In 1839 at Chatsworth, he had designed the Great Conservatory, the largest greenhouse in the world until its demolition in 1920. Later he built the Lily House to shelter the Victoria Regia tank. This glass house included many of the innovations that made the Crystal Palace possible. Paxton used the analogy of a table and tablecloth to explain the separate roles of structure and enclosure. He understood the nature and aesthetic possibilities of frame and enclosure better than many architects do today.

17. Joseph Paxton, Crystal Palace, London, England, 1851

*18. Joseph Paxton,
Crystal Palace, London,
England, 1851*

The Crystal Palace and the Great Exhibition were a great success. The building was open for just over five months and its attendance records—more than forty thousand people a day, with a total exceeding six million visitors—are proof of its mass appeal. These numbers would not mean much, however, had the building not been exciting and beautiful. It was beautiful—the record is clear on this matter—and this new beauty was appreciated and celebrated by people of all economic and intellectual classes. This building was the evidence that a radically new architecture, well suited to our time, was possible and capable of great beauty and excitement (fig. 18). Architecture was never the same afterward. The Crystal Palace was at least as radical a departure from the norms of architecture of its time as Manet's *Dejeuner sur l'Herbe* (1863), Cézanne's *Large Bathers* (1885), and Picasso's *Demoiselles d'Avignon* (1907) were from the norms of painting of their time.

Finally, a most important quality of Paxton's design is that it was built. It survived the conflicting pressures of many interest groups. It met an almost impossible schedule of two months for design and documentation and six months for construction, all within a very small budget. And yet it was built.

The modern past

An architecture does not develop along an even, clear course. The architecture of our time has changed direction, backtracked, split, and rejoined several times. International modernism offered a critique of previous modernist efforts and a new synthesis. We also have had critiques of international modernism and attempts at new paradigms. As is often the case, the critiques and new proposals are based on perceived disconnections between the dominant ideology and some aspects of reality. These critiques offer different and useful perspectives on the architecture of our time.

Robert Venturi's book *Complexity and Contradiction in Architecture* (1966) is a well-reasoned analysis of modernism's disconnection with architecture's own past. Venturi, almost single-handedly, brought back to life a rich tradition of previously ignored forms and architectural models. The book's great success was due not only to its cogent and original arguments but also to its legitimization of the basic desire to reconnect architecture with important aspects of its history.

Modernism started and grew as an outsiders' movement, but it is now the mainstream. Until World War II, the possibility of erecting major buildings with traditional systems of construction remained a viable alternative. Since then, that alternative has ceased to exist. What was daring for Paxton is inevitable for us.

I have the greatest admiration for the achievements of international modernism. But we can now put this episode in its proper place, free of the many distortions created by its own brilliant propaganda. The messianic character of early international modernism may have been necessary to galvanize the profession, give modernity a unified front, and convert the unbelievers. The architectural vacuum created by the Great Depression and World War II was followed by a postwar construction boom that propelled international modernism beyond anybody's expectations, perhaps too fast. We can now go back over international modernism's many experiments and try to learn from its successes and failures. We can adopt those innovations that worked and discard or alter those that did not. We do not have to wait until the failure of an experiment is

19. *Michel de Klerk,*
Eigen Haard Housing,
Amsterdam, Holland,
1917

20. *Le Corbusier, Unité*
d'Habitation, Marseilles,
France, 1952

*21. Eliel Saarinen,
Cranbrook Academy
of Art, Bloomfield Hills,
Michigan, 1926–42*

*22. Walter Gropius,
Bauhaus Buildings,
Dessau, Germany,
1926*

so notorious that it has to be blown up to reconsider its underlying idea. (This happened in 1972 to Minoru Yamasaki's 1955 Pruitt-Igoe housing complex in Saint Louis, Missouri. In this case the design was based on the belief that residential towers set in a park are an ideal way to live.)

We can reexamine not only the results of the experiments of international modernism but also those of all other architects who grappled with problems that relate to ours today. We may conclude that de Klerk left us with more livable and urbane models for public housing than Le Corbusier did (figs. 19, 20), or that we can learn more about high buildings from John Wellborn Root or Raymond Hood than from Mies van der Rohe. Or that if we have to plan the buildings for a design school, the Cranbrook Academy of Art may be a better model than the Bauhaus (figs. 21, 22). These are all useful precedents and each one can teach us something of value.

Postmodernism

There is no movement or ideology without flaws. And probably there is no movement that does not offer some useful insights. We should consider carefully and with skepticism every idea that attracts us and should also not reject any serious proposal without a sympathetic appraisal. Artistic movements compete not on a life-or-death battleground but in a marketplace of ideas, and most of them offer some elements of value. Postmodernism represented a major challenge to the prevailing orthodoxy. It was introduced with shock tactics and passionately counterattacked, which did not allow for calm discussion of its merits. But postmodernism's effect on architecture and its popular acceptance were too great for it to be dismissed as superficial fashion. The phenomenon of postmodernism contains some useful lessons for us.

There are three views of postmodernism that interest me. The first view is the best known, because it is what caught the attention of the press and what its detractors single out for criticism: postmodernism as an aesthetic movement that engaged in indulgent facade designs, anti-modernism, and inappropriate historicism. This represents some but not all aspects of postmodernism.

The second view of postmodernism derives from a literal interpretation of its name. It defines a position in a temporal sequence. Because this meaning is useful, it has been borrowed by other artistic and intellectual disciplines. In this sense, today we are all postmodernists. Modernism presented itself as a revolution, and today we practice well after its revolutionary period. Post-revolutionary implies that the revolution was won; it is over. Now is the moment to make a new world on that basis, and slogans and dogmatism are unnecessary. This is a valid position.

The third view of postmodernism deserves a more careful appraisal. It interprets postmodernism as a correction that confirms the universality of modernism and offers a useful reevaluation of its principles and practices. Postmodernism cast light on key disconnections, especially the disconnection between international modernism and our cities. This disconnection was caused in part by Le Corbusier's personal dislike of the traditional city and his ambition to create a new paradigm, a new city. Several attempts to implement his ideas, such as Chandigarh and Brasilia, have produced cities less livable and less adaptable than traditional ones. The antiurban bias of international modernism was reinforced by its theoretical focus on the inner nature of the individual building: the honest expression of structure, function, and industrial materials. This concern was laudable but, in its insistence, left little room to consider the building's role as maker of public space, including streets, or as a part of the larger and more important whole that is the city. International modernist buildings rarely contribute to the form or structure of the traditional city—the only successful model we have—and we also observe that buildings conceived as autonomous art objects have not succeeded in giving coherent form to any kind of new city.

Postmodernism reminded us that buildings have symbolic roles to play, that character may be more important than aesthetic composition, and that we perceive buildings not only with our eyes but also with our memory. Finally, postmodernism challenged international modernism's disconnection with the history of architecture. This disconnection was harmful in itself, cutting off our own roots, but it also sanctioned an attitude of ignoring precedents, a reluctance to learn from experience. We still seem to believe that armed with an architectural degree and a few facts we are qualified to solve any problem from scratch.

This critical aspect of postmodernism was essential in gaining it the widespread support it received. However, it should be noted that the shortcomings criticized by postmodernism apply only to international modernism. They do not apply to the larger or inclusive modernism for which I argue. Simply accepting the legitimacy of the wide range of approaches and models created by all modern architects since the 1850s frees us of the ideological limitations of international modernism. Defining modernism correctly makes it unnecessary to seek answers in inappropriate historical models or in forms based on obsolete construction systems. And, with cleared heads and conscience, we can honestly engage in designing suitable buildings for our time.

I learned architecture at the University of Tucumán in Argentina (1944-49), at the University of Illinois (1952-54), and during my apprenticeship with Eero Saarinen (1954-64). My mentors were modern architects of the "second generation." They believed their role was to transmit and implement the principles of architecture as they had been defined by the founders of international modernism. During my formative years, the founders were still very much alive and busy producing new work that sometimes challenged earlier understanding of their positions. My fellow students and I sensed that we were in the midst of a momentous change and that we were expected to participate in bringing it to fruition.

It was not easy for second-generation modern architects, working in the shadow of their acknowledged masters, to chart their own course and to react to their own time. Most of them felt that they had to learn from the work of the first generation and elaborate on their models. The independence displayed in much of the work of Eero Saarinen and Louis Kahn is thus all the more admirable; given their position in the sequence, the tentative nature of their exploratory early years is understandable. The case of Eero Saarinen is particularly tragic because he died at fifty-one, just as his career was gaining great momentum. If Louis Kahn had died at the same age, he would not have built any of the projects for which he is best known.

During my school years, I experienced two interpretations of international modernism. At school in Tucumán, modernism meant, above all, logic and social purpose. The writings of Le Corbusier were the primary guide. For students at the time, urbanism was on a higher plane than architecture, the plan was always the generator, and the elevations were the result (the term "facade" was frowned upon as formalistic). The most important design problem was public housing, and the solution was expected to be conceived in monoblocks, based on Le Corbusier's Unité d'Habitation. Building form was the result of straightforward (or clever) functional arrangements. Reinforced concrete was the preferred modern material, but also accepted were materials and systems derived from the vernacular, since they represented the unaffected response to available technology. My first "modern" design, in my first year of school, was a one-room house for a sugar-cane laborer that I designed with stuccoed brick walls painted white with a dark blue wainscot, and a red tile roof.

At the University of Illinois, I encountered a different view of modernism. The emphasis was on style and on the designs of the masters as formal models. I do not remember anyone discussing modernist theories. Le Corbusier was known, but he had no influence on the designs produced at the school at that time. Gropius was important on the East Coast, but in the Midwest and soon in the whole country, Mies van der Rohe's influence was unmatched. Plans, elevations, and structure were shaped by "the grid," and steel and glass were the preferred materials. My first design at Illinois was an expandable factory.

Many doors open or close for us depending on the moment we enter the artistic sequence. I started my career during a critical period in modern architecture. Through my years of learning, I was exposed to a wide range of experiences and I was duly impressed with the works of the masters of international modernism. I have not lost my admiration for their achievements, but after some time I came to realize that, although the changes in our world were real, I did not have to accept unquestioningly other people's interpretation of the nature of the changes or their version of the proper architecture for our time.

CONSTRUCTION

*Architecture is to create moving emotional
relationships with inert materials.*
—Le Corbusier, 1923

The connection of construction technology with architecture is most intimate because it affects the conception of every building. Its effect on architecture is two-pronged: on our design practice and on our ideology. When only some aspects of construction change, we adapt our designs to them. When the change in construction technologies is fundamental, we must reconsider the nature of architecture itself.

Construction and practice

Construction sets the limits of what is physically possible. In the Middle Ages, the designers of Gothic cathedrals stretched the possibilities of load-bearing stone technology to enclose higher and higher spaces. Beauvais Cathedral has the highest Gothic vault ever built (157 feet 6 inches). It had to be held together by iron rods. Its nave was never erected and its spire of five hundred feet toppled in 1573. There were no higher Gothic cathedrals attempted after Beauvais. In our time, we have built as high as 120 stories, and we may soon build up to 150 or 180 stories. Today, however, height is limited by the economics of construction and by the still-restricted ability of mechanical systems to respond to human physiological needs and tolerances, not by the strength of materials.

Construction limits are important and ever present. But architectural form is affected more by the less obvious, yet relentless pressure on almost every project to adapt the design toward the practical center of construction possibilities. The practical center is that point where, for the same level of quality, buildings cost less (per unit of area or volume), can be built faster, and face fewer risks. We can design away from the center but this requires more generous budgets and other allowances from our clients. Even then, the pull of the practical center affects most decisions. The center is not necessarily conservative; it is also the zone in which new technologies allow buildings to achieve objectives (larger spaces, higher standards of function or comfort) that older construction technologies cannot provide. When the practical center moves, the practice of architecture moves with it.

Construction and ideology

Fundamental changes in construction technology can redirect the course of architecture and force us to reconsider its underpinning ideology. Although many developments led to the ideology of modernism, modern architecture has defined and justified itself primarily in terms of a new construction technology or, more accurately, by claiming to provide a clear response to fundamental and irreversible changes in how our buildings are built.

There have been, and still are, several construction systems using a variety of materials that have produced many great buildings, but in the Western world the forms of the buildings and the ideology of modernism were affected primarily by the shift in construction systems from *load-bearing masonry* to *frame and enclosure*. This shift is seen most clearly in the replacement of classicism by modernism as a dominant aesthetic system. By dominant, I mean the construction system normally used for the large and important buildings of a society, the buildings that set the tone and introduce formal changes that are then imitated in lesser structures.

The shift from load-bearing masonry to frame and enclosure did not happen overnight. The transition took place slowly and unevenly over a period of some one hundred years. Frame and enclosure began to be used in architecture in the mid-nineteenth century, but the change in construction systems was not complete until World War II, many years after modernism had developed its universal ideology. Today, we are in a position to evaluate what actually changed in construction technology and perhaps reconsider the ideological basis of our architectural responses.

Stone masonry

The traditions of architectural design and of building construction are so interrelated that at times they appear to be the same. Yet design grows from construction, and changes in the traditions of architectural design—such as from Romanesque to Gothic to Renaissance—occur less slowly than they do in construction. In much of the world, the main system of construction remained basically the same from the time of Sumer until the twentieth century. This system was the tradition of load-bearing masonry. Walls, and sometimes roofs, were built of earth, adobe, brick, volcanic cements, and even wooden logs. Some of these structures (for example, Hagia Sophia, 537) were very sophisticated technologically, had great beauty, and strongly affected the development of architecture. The paragon of load-bearing structures, however, has been stone construction. Since ancient Egypt, stone masonry has been the dominant system of construction in the Western world.

Stone masonry buildings were erected in layers of stone blocks, which formed the walls and supported the roofs. Projecting rows of stones were carved into moldings. The walls were heavy, and stone lintels allowed only for small openings. Stone walls were thick and openings were deep. Stone arches made larger openings possible. The centering stone of the arch was the keystone. When a wall was made of irregular or softer stones, harder and more durable stones were used in the corners and at the edges of openings. These became quoins. Columns were hefty and not far apart. A rich play of light and shadow existed in the very nature of these thick, modulated stone walls and columns. Much of the aesthetic vocabulary of classical architecture grew out of the possibilities and limitations of load-bearing stone construction.

Throughout the history of load-bearing construction, stone was a special, respected material. The most gifted architects constantly renewed the forms of stone construction, which were then imitated not only in stone but also in brick, plaster, and wood. The tradition of stone construction was at the root of Egyptian, Greek, Roman, Indian, Mayan, Gothic, Renaissance, and other architectures. It set their limits and defined their opportunities, establishing a strong kinship among them. The Temple of Ammon at Luxor (fourteenth century B.C.E.), the House of Turtles in Uxmal, Mexico (tenth century C.E.), the Temple of Sulamani in Pagan, Burma (twelfth century), Notre Dame de Paris (twelfth and thirteenth centuries), and the Palazzo Pitti in Florence (fifteenth through seventeenth centuries) all belong to the same family of formal possibilities (figs. 23–27). Their forms are unlike those of other traditions, such as the timber construction of Scandinavia, Russia, and Japan (figs. 28–30).

Stone masonry was first challenged in the second half of the nineteenth century, and alternative technologies became more and more

Opposite
23. House of Turtles,
Uxmal, Mexico, c. 900

24. Temple of
Sulamani, Pagan,
Burma, twelfth century

25. Cathedral of Notre
Dame, Paris, France,
1163–1250

accepted over the years. However, stone masonry did not lose its preeminent status until World War II. Many civic and academic buildings in America were built of stone in the 1930s, just before the war. After the war, stone masonry construction practically disappeared. It lost its dominance for several reasons. The first was practical—industrial materials and processes offer greater heights, longer spans, faster construction, and better insulation. The second was economic—carved load-bearing stone is slow, labor intensive, and requires a very skilled work force. The third was social—stone masonry depended on a hierarchical social system in which the lower classes provided a continuous supply of able workers willing to spend long years in a difficult apprenticeship only to end up as laborers. Today, similarly capable individuals can become architects, or lawyers or doctors. Stone buildings are still possible, and some are being built. But load-bearing stone is no longer a living tradition shaping our most important buildings and being renewed by the minds of the best architects of our time.

Carved-stone masonry had a long life, roughly contemporaneous with horse-drawn transportation. Both became dominant systems some seven thousand years ago and disappeared as competitive systems by

26. Temple of Ammon, Luxor, Egypt, c. 1300 B.C.E.

27. Fancelli-Ammanati-Parigi, Palazzo Pitti, Florence, Italy, 1465, 1570, 1640

28. *Stave Church,*
Borgund, Norway,
c. 1150

29. *Yukushiji Temple,*
Japan, eighth century

Opposite
30. *Church of the*
Transfiguration,
Kozlyatero, Russia,
1756

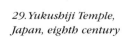

31. *Wedding procession, London, England, 1947*

World War II. Both systems have great visceral appeal and continue to be used on special occasions, when ceremony requires (fig. 31).

Frame and enclosure

Today we have a new dominant construction system, that of frame and enclosure. A frame of steel or reinforced concrete supports not only floors and roof but also the walls that enclose a building. The enclosure is usually made of several thin layers, each with a specific purpose: exterior finish, physical protection, thermal insulation, waterproofing, vapor barrier, and interior finish. One of the arguments for the inevitability of modernism has been that the aesthetic systems appropriate to a tradition of construction based on the assemblage of a skeleton structure with a lightweight enclosure must be radically different from the systems of forms that developed from a tradition of construction based on stone masonry. The argument is an old one, although it did not become fully valid until the 1950s, when load-bearing stone construction ceased to be a practical alternative.

The impact of frame-and-enclosure technology on architectural theory is evident in Le Corbusier's "five points for a new architecture" of 1927.
Four of the points—free plan, horizontal windows, free facade, and pilo-
tis—are direct expressions of the new possibilities offered by frame-and-
enclosure construction. Only the fifth point—roof garden—was possible
with load-bearing construction.

Frame and enclosure is now the dominant construction technology, but
there are alternative, if limited, construction systems. Wall-bearing reinforced
concrete has been used in several distinguished modern buildings, such as Le
Corbusier's monastery of La Tourette in Eveux (1960), Louis Kahn's Salk Institute in San Diego (1965), and much of Tadao Ando's work. Its appeal derives,
to a large extent, from its re-creation of the durable, thick, heavy walls of
stone construction. For smaller buildings, wood and brick construction systems remain widely available and competitive.

Some building systems or some materials may have greater appeal for
us than others. We may see them as more "modern." But there is no right
or wrong construction system. If a building system has survived and is
affordable, it is appropriate to our time. All existing construction systems
are contemporary. The diverse qualities of the buildings we admire suggest that modernity, the architecture of our time, does not depend on the
use, or avoidance, of specific materials. We need only look at the use of
heavy stone walls in Le Corbusier's Maison de Mandrot (1932) or the
rough brick walls punctured by windows in Alvar Aalto's Baker House at
MIT (1948) or the pitched tile roofs of Louis Kahn's Trenton Bath House
(1956). We are fortunate to have viable alternative construction traditions
because they give wider range to our architectural voices and provide us
with the necessary tools with which to reconnect new buildings with old
ones. Perhaps the only reliable and objective connection between architectural form and our time, defining modernity, is the authentic expression of contemporary construction. Forms and styles are important to all
designers, and we are more attracted to the work of those architects who
have wrestled with aesthetic issues similar to those that we confront. If we
depend only on aesthetic qualities to accept a building as modern, we
reduce a most important architectural development into a style, which is
then subject to the vagaries of fashion.

The Greek temple

Styles are not the substance of an architecture, but when an architecture responds appropriately to existing technology, not all forms are valid. Because the forms of load-bearing stone construction are still cherished by many, classicists have raised the questions "Why can't we replicate the forms of one construction system with the technology of another? Didn't the stone forms of the Greek temple derive from an earlier tradition of wood construction?" These are good questions because they address the logic of forms in architecture. And the historical forms remain relevant because they compose much of our urban context, offer us artistic precedents, and still linger in our collective memory.

To answer these questions, based on the continuity of forms in Greek temples, we can start by first noting that the characteristics of heavy timber construction for short-span structures are not dissimilar from post-and-lintel stone construction. Second, Greek temples were sacred buildings, shaped by their rituals, and the continuity of forms responded to the continued demands of a living religion. Third, and most important, the architectural forms of the Greek temple are fully consistent with its stone nature; there is nothing false in them; only the formal elements suitable to stone architecture were retained from an earlier wood construction tradition. When we are in the presence of these temples, it is only the stone that matters. At that critical moment, the wood precedent is simply a historical curiosity with no architectural reality.

Today we face a new condition. The present technology is radically different from the previous one. The chain of architectural forms that grew from a living religion was broken and abandoned by the Renaissance. And our international society does not have a common religion.

An architecture grows only when it is based on a living tradition of building construction. Frame and enclosure, the now dominant system of construction, is new, and its characteristics are still developing. Whether we like it or not, we must develop the forms for a still-young architecture. The tradition of construction is given to us; how we architects use it to give life and soul to our architecture is our responsibility.

Permanence

Buildings outlive their makers and sometimes they outlive the societies that required them. In most cultures buildings became a vehicle for expressing the human desire to extend the reach of our lives. Available technologies have colored our attitudes about permanence. In countries in which stone technology was dominant, important buildings were built to be as robust as possible, with the thought that their mass and weight would permit them to endure. They could defy time. The most successful products of this aspiration are still the great pyramids at Gizeh (fig. 32). Societies that built with masonry came to equate permanence with massiveness. In countries that built with wood, buildings could be made to last only if they were continuously repaired. Wood buildings cannot defy time but depend on life to survive. The most sophisticated example of this approach is the Ise Shrine in Mei prefecture, Japan (fig. 33). The temple has remained unchanged for thirteen centuries, relying on a continuous dedication that has rebuilt it every twenty years. Every twenty years the temple is new and, at the same time, many centuries old.

32. Great Pyramids, Gizeh, Egypt, c. 2700 B.C.E.

33. Shrine of Ise, Mei prefecture, Japan, seventh century

Appearance and reality

Load-bearing stone as a reasonable construction alternative ended only recently, in the mid-twentieth century. The aesthetic qualities of this system are so ingrained in our culture that it has been difficult to adjust to their loss, and we have seen many efforts to re-create the old cherished forms in other materials, such as plastic casts and thin stone veneers on hollow walls. Unfortunately, without a direct connection to the underlying technology, all these efforts will remain fruitless. Form-giving needs to continually test itself against the possibilities of construction or it degenerates.

People expect a basic consistency between the appearance and the reality of what they see. We all can tolerate a certain level of misinformation or deception, and, if it is clever, we are amused by it, but on the whole we want the world to be coherent and truthful. We may all enjoy and even admire well-made wax fruits and silk flowers, but the pleasure we derive lies in discovering their artifice, not in being fooled by them. In our daily lives we all prefer real fruits and flowers.

Many artistic manifestations can be, and often are expected to be, beyond reality. This is fitting for arts such as painting, sculpture, poetry, music, literature, theater, and film. I can choose when to experience such arts, or not to experience them at all. I know that in them I enter worlds that are not my everyday world. Almost all architecture exists in our unavoidable everyday world. Even the glorious exceptions become part of normal life. That is why people expect the buildings that make our environment to be basically what they claim to be. Basically is enough. They do not need to be truthful in every detail. That is an unachievable standard, in conflict with other worthy goals, such as beauty or contextuality.

Huts

Humanity has developed only a few basic construction technologies. The buildings generated by each technology are often stylistically different from one another when erected by various cultures, but they share basic formal characteristics. Load-bearing masonry is one such technology. Another is the lightweight hut. The term *hut* is applied to several building types. Many of these usages are derogatory, reflecting our disdain for modest constructions and nomadic cultures. I will adopt one common usage, suitable for architectural discourse, to describe a basic and universal type of construction.

Huts are one-room buildings made with frames of branches or cane, covered with thin, flexible enclosures of grass, leaves, skins, or textiles. Huts were built all over the world, and many are still built today. Huts are not sturdy proto-Greek temples, as the Abbé Laugier suggested in 1755 (fig. 34), and they are not primitive. Huts can be handsome, and some are very beautiful. They are sophisticated and adaptable structures that probably provide more shelter per unit of effort and are more ecologically benign than any other form of construction. Hut technology is the longest-lasting construction system the world has had.

34. *Abbé Marc-Antoine Laugier, "Primitive Hut." From* Essai sur l'architecture, *1775*

35. *Grass house, North Rhodesia (now Zimbabwe)*

Huts share several characteristics. They are lightweight frame-and-enclo-sure constructions and are often portable. Their walls are thin, continuous surfaces forming volumes. Walls and roof are one. Architectural expression is in the silhouette and not in the facade composition (they rarely have a "facade"). Huts are modest constructions, seldom decorated; when they are, decoration is two-dimensional, provided by the texture of the building materials or applied as paintings or weavings to the enclosing surface. Throughout human history, widely separated groups of people, mostly nomadic, in all climatic zones, developed their own styles of huts and gave them names such as tepees, yurts, and black tents. All, however, had similar formal traits that grew naturally from the shared system of construction (figs. 35–40).

36. Grass house, Brazil

37. Kanuri house,
Nigeria

38. Turkemen yurt,
Afghanistan

39. Blackfoot tepees,
Canada

40. Sambar black tent,
Eritrea

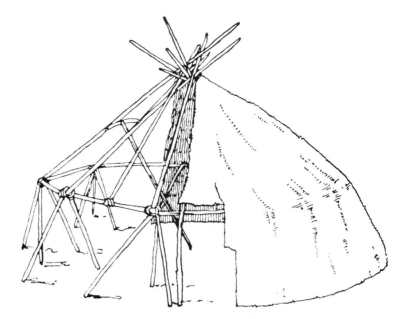

41. Chukchee kot under construction, Siberia

42. Cesar Pelli at Gruen Associates, Pacific Design Center under construction, Los Angeles County, California, 1974

The tradition of hut construction bears many conceptual similarities to our present-day system of frame and enclosure (figs. 41, 42). These similarities suggest that today we are somehow reconnecting with a very ancient building tradition, older than stone masonry. As with huts, our system of construction is based on an open frame that supports a lightweight enclosure. Exterior form is achieved with a two-dimensional surface that describes a three-dimensional volume, although in our case wall and roof are usually distinct elements. Decoration is most easily achieved as two-dimensional changes of color or texture. These two construction systems are not closely related technologies. But their conceptual similarities can help us to better understand our dominant technology of construction as we endeavor to interpret it through our architecture.

Construction and form

The work of H. H. Richardson in the mid- to late nineteenth century provides us with useful examples of the relationship between building form and construction reality. Richardson was an eclectic architect who practiced during a period of transition in construction technologies. He was also a sensitive artist, and his forms had a close relationship to the materials and construction systems he employed.

The Marshall Field Wholesale Store in Chicago (1887) is a useful example precisely because it was impure: it had metal columns and beams, and exterior stone walls that supported little more than themselves (fig. 43). At that time, masonry was beginning to be replaced by skeleton structures of cast iron or steel, though carved stone was still widely available. These two systems were apparent in the building and gave life to the architecture. In relation to the size and height of this building, the stone wall was thin and open, and together with the glass, it expressed a single, crisp enclosure of space. Richardson also took full advantage of the qualities of carved stone, and the "stoniness" of the building was unquestionable. However, when he designed the Stoughton House (1883) in a "purer" construction of wood frame and shingles, he used a different aesthetic approach that expressed the lightweight, ephemeral quality of the structure, and the openings were

43. H. H. Richardson,
Marshall Field
Wholesale Store,
Chicago, Illinois, 1887

44. H. H. Richardson,
Stoughton House,
Cambridge,
Massachusetts, 1883

45. H. H. Richardson, Allegheny County Courthouse and Jail, Pittsburgh, Pennsylvania, 1888

shaped as if cut with scissors from a lightweight material (fig. 44). When he designed in load-bearing stone, as he did in the Allegheny County Courthouse and Jail (1888) the stone was thick and heavy and his arches spoke of weight and craftsmanship (fig. 45). Richardson considered the Marshall Field Store and the Allegheny Courthouse his two best designs. In his work, as in most good architecture, there is a close relationship between form and substance.

46. Richard Rogers,
Lloyd's of London
Building, London,
England, 1984

Aesthetic expression

Construction occupies a well-earned place of honor in the modernist pantheon. Buildings through the ages have naturally expressed the way they were built. International modernism went further, and telling the story of a building's construction often became the motivation for and justification of its design. Several aesthetic strategies have claimed to best express the essence of today's construction, including the Bauhaus school, constructivism, brutalism, and the influential designs of Ludwig Mies van der Rohe and Buckminster Fuller. High-tech design is more recent and still developing. Its examination can tell us something about how we perceive buildings and about the shifting relationship between technology and aesthetics. We may start by noting that there is no high technology in architecture. True high technology is very expensive and based on sophisticated research, such as that for interplanetary probes or microchips. Buildings are coarse affairs that do not need and cannot afford such specialized precision. The high-tech look is usually achieved with increased craftsmanship, as in Richard Rogers's design for the Lloyd's of London building (1984; fig. 46).

The justification for a high-tech expression is in the realm of aesthetics. There is not just one kind of beauty in buildings. We experience beauty with our senses, but also with our reason and memory. A classical design, such as the Boston Public Library (1895) by McKim, Mead and White (fig. 47) is perceived as beautiful not only because its forms are pleasing but also because it is built in a reassuring style with an exalted lineage. Mies van der Rohe's Lake Shore Drive apartments in Chicago (1951) are masterfully detailed and proportioned (fig. 48), but more important in his American work is the intellectual beauty conveyed by the Cartesian grid of structure and mullions. The buildings' role as early models of venerated architectural postulates contributes much to our perception of their aesthetic value. Some buildings, like Frank Lloyd Wright's Fallingwater (1939), fascinate us with their daring forms and the way they appropriate the energy of nature in their design (fig. 49). The appeal of other buildings may be in their unex-

47. McKim, Mead and White, Public Library, Boston, Massachusetts, 1895

Opposite
48. Ludwig Mies van
der Rohe, Lake Shore
Drive Apartments,
Chicago, Illinois, 1951

49. Frank Lloyd Wright,
Fallingwater, Bear
Run, Pennsylvania,
1939

*50. Frank O. Gehry,
Guggenheim Museum
Bilbao, Bilbao, Spain,
1997*

pected, beautiful forms that create associations with other arts—such as
Frank Gehry's Guggenheim Museum in Bilbao (1997; fig. 50)—or in their
intellectual virtuosity—such as Peter Eisenman's Houses I to X (1967–75;
fig. 51). Some tall buildings, such as Mies van der Rohe's Seagram tower in
New York (1958; fig. 52), are esteemed for their minimalist simplicity, but
other tall buildings, such as the towers of Antoni Gaudí's Sagrada Familia in
Barcelona (1926; fig. 53), are admired for their exuberant forms and rich
complexity of details. High-tech buildings appeal to us with the image of a
more sophisticated future world combined with the feeling of a refined
industrial craft executed in fine materials. It is a feeling akin to that of seeing and wanting to touch a beautifully crafted camera, rifle, or racing bicy-

51. Peter Eisenman,
House X, 1975.
Unbuilt project

cle. If Norman Foster's work is compared with that of earlier architects—
Albert Kahn's factories of the 1920s and 1930s and the house that Charles
and Ray Eames built for themselves in 1949, for example—the difference is
obvious. These wonderful buildings also derive their beauty from the intelligent use of the latest construction systems, but they are too direct, too
industrial, to be labeled high-tech (fig. 54–56).

It is difficult to measure buildings that have different aesthetic reso-
nances. Each requires its own yardstick. This is one reason why the results
of architectural competitions can be so disconcerting. The judges may
have used a different yardstick than the one participants and observers
thought appropriate for the problem.

54. Norman Foster,
Carré d'Art, Nîmes,
France, 1993

55. Charles and Ray
Eames, Eames House,
Santa Monica,
California, 1949

56. Albert Kahn,
Dodge Half-Ton Truck
Plant, near Detroit,
Michigan, 1938

Our task

The connection between design and building remains as essential as ever. But the construction technology of our time is complex, and its qualities are not as easily understood as were those of load-bearing systems. Also, because late-twentieth-century construction is not based on handicrafts, much of the making of buildings (in factories and assembly shops) is physically and emotionally removed from the designer. This was not so with earlier craft-based technologies. Today, each one of us must make a special effort to understand the subtleties of our technology and to respond appropriately with our designs.

Most of the great and beautiful buildings of Western architecture were built of load-bearing masonry. Their forms contain most of our architectural memories. They still give form and character to many of our cities. Yet the technology that gave them life is now obsolete. Today we have new construction systems with which to make architecture. As always, our only option is to understand the possibilities of the technologies available to us. It is our task to develop, with our technology, an architecture as rich, meaningful, and loved as was the architecture of stone.

I learned in school that the honest expression of the nature of construction was an essential characteristic of a healthy architecture. Later, I came to see that it also provides the strongest connection between our architecture and our time independent of style. This understanding has guided me well through my professional life.

When I joined DMJM, I started to produce my own designs. I had to work with very tight budgets, short schedules, and minimal client support. I could not hope to refine or even match the physical qualities of the buildings I admired. These circumstances, along with my interest in the theoretical aspects of construction and modernity, led me, together with Anthony Lumsden, to reconsider the nature of thin enclosures and their artistic possibilities. In 1965, Lumsden and I designed the adventuresome, sculpted Federal Building for the United States General Services Administration (GSA) in Lawndale, California. It was clad with reflective

57. Cesar Pelli and
Anthony Lumsden
at DMJM, Federal
Building, Lawndale,
California. Model,
1965

58. Cesar Pelli and
Anthony Lumsden
at DMJM, Federal
Building, Lawndale,
California, 1973

glass and aluminum panels and was too ambitious for our budget,
dependent on details and craftsmanship we could not afford. The building (which was not built until 1973) fell short of our design intentions
as we had expressed them in drawings and models (figs. 57, 58).

Our second attempt at a thin enclosure, all in glass, was modest,
economical, and successful. The Century City Medical Center, designed
in 1966 and built in 1969, was, I believe, the first high-rise building ever
built as a pure prism of uniformly gridded glass, carried from ground
to skyline (fig. 59). The design took advantage of a relatively recent and
economical product: ceramic-coated glass. We used tinted glass for the
windows and ceramic-coated glass, matching the color of the windows,

for the opaque portions of the buildings. The glass was held in a small, regular grid of the thinnest and shallowest mullions possible. There were good precedents for this approach, such as Lever House (1952). But this design challenged the then prevalent aesthetic advocated by Mies van der Rohe, in which deep mullions expressed structure and order. Our intention was to emphasize the continuity of the enclosure and we did not want the mullions to interrupt the surface or obscure the reflective qualities of the glass. The total assemblage was inexpensive and handsome, and it expressed our ideas with clarity. The Medical Center is a plain and modest structure, but it was well received by the international architectural press, and, because of its practical advantages, it was the first of many buildings designed with similar qualities. This building was for me the beginning of one path of exploration in architecture. It is an aesthetic search for an architecture that expresses, with clarity and beauty, the nature of today's buildings as lightweight envelopes supported by an inner (protected) frame.

At Gruen Associates, I designed the San Bernardino City Hall, which was completed in 1972 (fig. 60). Its design was more ambitious than that for the Medical Center, but this time I carefully targeted my ambition to get the most of what was possible, not more. As in the Medical Center, the exterior wall is made of a uniform grid of closely spaced, very thin mullions holding tinted vision glass and matching opaque panels of ceramic glass. The City Hall has a strong sculptural form, but unlike the Federal Building, which depended on metal panels and compound curves, here the all-glass form was shaped with straight facets. The taut surface flows under and around the faceted planes, expressing the continuity of the enclosure and creating a dynamic form with constantly changing reflections.

The design of the 1975 Pacific Design Center in Los Angeles County (now the city of West Hollywood) allowed me to carry the idea of a three-dimensional volume defined by a two-dimensional surface a step further. Like the two buildings just described, the aesthetic appeal of the Pacific Design Center rests on the intellectual order of the wrapping grid and the play of changing reflections on the glass surface. But here, the visual qualities of the enclosure are modified by the use of a strong

*Opposite
59. Cesar Pelli and Anthony Lumsden at DMJM, Century City Medical Center, Los Angeles, California, 1969*

color. The deep blue of the ceramic glass has an immediate effect on the senses, changing the perceptual balance of the architecture. It makes the form stronger and at the same time more approachable. The building was soon nicknamed "the blue whale" (fig. 61). Later I designed a green building (completed in 1988) as a companion to the blue one, and planned a red one to complete the composition (fig. 62).

For the design of the Museum Tower in New York (completed in 1984) I explored the aesthetic possibilities of expressing internal functions on the glass envelope. The exterior walls of the tower describe floors, windows, and the changing rhythms of the dwelling functions inside with several colors of ceramic glass (fig. 63). I designed the residential Four Leaf Towers in Houston (completed in 1982) with similar aesthetic intentions, but using a color palette appropriate to the Houston environment. Glass towers are associated with office buildings. In these two projects, I wanted to design simple and taut glass towers that looked residential. The color modulations make the internal purpose visible on the exterior.

Opposite
60. Cesar Pelli at Gruen Associates, City Hall, San Bernardino, California, 1972

In later projects, I expanded my explorations with thin enclosures by using other, less obvious, contemporary materials, while allowing them to be read as the taut and light skins they are. The American Embassy in Tokyo (1975) has a wall of precast concrete panels, as stipulated by the U.S. State Department. Herring Hall at Rice University in Houston is enclosed in brick veneer, as are most buildings on the campus. The World Financial Center in New York City (1987) is clad in preassembled panels of thin veneer stone and glass. I enjoyed designing with these diverse materials and trying to make them clearly express their role of thin enclosures.

Respecting the nature of today's construction technology made my designs buildable and economical, and connected my architecture with our time in the clearest manner I knew how. I have had other preoccupations in my architecture, and they have all affected my designs to different degrees, according to the circumstances of each project. No artist has unlimited abilities. I believe that, given my own limits, several lines of exploration, on different substantial issues, have given greater adaptability and depth to my architecture. My designs would have been poorer, and fewer of them would have been built, if I had pursued a single overriding goal in my architecture.

61. Cesar Pelli at
Gruen Associates,
Pacific Design Center,
Los Angeles County,
California, 1975

62. Cesar Pelli &
Associates, Pacific
Design Center: Phases
I, II, and III, West
Hollywood, California.
Model

63. Cesar Pelli &
Associates, Museum
Tower, New York,
New York, 1984

PLACE

No aspect of architecture requires as much sensitivity as designing a building to connect well with its place. Much of the beauty and power of the Potala Palace, Mont Saint-Michel, Kiomizu, Machu Picchu, and Rockefeller Center (figs. 64–68) comes from designs that resonate with and amplify the qualities of their unique places.

The physical rootedness of buildings characterizes the art of architecture. Today, other artists are also designing "site-specific" pieces. In these designs, knowingly or not, they approximate architecture, and their work acquires architectural qualities that reaffirm the value of an art that belongs to its place.

Our time and our construction systems reflect new conditions that changed our architecture. The need to connect a building with its place remains unaltered.

Parts of something larger

Sites do not exist by themselves. They are part of something larger: a natural or urban context. Similarly, the buildings we design do not exist by themselves. They become part of a landscape, an ecology, a neighborhood, a city. Natural landscapes and urban settings present different design opportunities but all places require sensitive responses. A building in a landscape not only enjoys views but also becomes part of the view and of the character of a place. A building on an open site affects its ecology, increasing the amount of impervious surface and changing the patterns of drainage. If the site is in a remote area, it may require extending the infrastructure of roads and services; it may inhibit the migration of wild animals and have other effects on the environment. Today, most new buildings are built within the context of other buildings. They may be in a central city, an edge city, a suburb, or a campus, but the condition is "urban." The new building will become a part of a larger ensemble of buildings. A new building may be handsome in itself, but, more important, it will join other buildings and will make the total better or worse by its presence.

I admire many buildings for their own independent qualities. But I reserve my greatest admiration for those buildings that move me not only with their beauty but also with the way that they energize and gain energy from their particular place in a city or landscape. When the relationship of building to place is awkward, I question the design, even when I find the building beautiful in itself.

Opposite
64. Potala Palace,
Lhasa, Tibet, 1695

People care for the places in which they live, and often, through laws and regulations, they require architects to respect the urban qualities they prize. Design controls, if they have wide public support, can be an effective way to create or preserve the special character of a place. One may or may not agree with the aesthetic or social goals of communities such as Carmel, Santa Barbara, and Nantucket, but there is no doubt that each of them has succeeded in preserving and enhancing an architectural character and lifestyle that they value. At other times, design controls are only capricious roadblocks with no good purpose. In any case, such regulations are proof that society recognizes the impact architecture can have on our environment and our lives.

Design and context

Designs that are sensitive to their place are often responsive not only to their sites and neighborhoods but also to their region, with its particular character, tradition of building, and history. We find these qualities pri-

marily in older buildings, because in the past, place was a strong determinant of design. Most construction materials were found nearby. Craftsmen could travel, but normally stayed within small regions, sharing skills and designs of aesthetic details. Public consensus on what was architecturally desirable was also regional. Architects could not stray far from the norms of a place. That is why we easily recognize, and enjoy, the regional architectural character of Tuscany, the Aegean islands, or New England.

Today, the direct influence of place on architectural decisions is very weak, and the connection to place is too easily ignored. Natural materials and manufactured building components come from all over the world. Local labor provides only the simplest of crafts. Global communications systems have disseminated a jumble of formal models. These changes have been, on the whole, liberating, and I do not yearn for the old days. However, now that place no longer has the strength to express itself, we need to make a special effort if we want our buildings to connect with their locations.

When I design a building to fit into its context, I try to identify the temporal center of the place: the period when the structures that give it its character were built. This is a personal assessment, to help me as I design. I form my impression by observing the place and its buildings, and by talking with those who live there. We may or may not want our design to be consonant with this quality, but if we understand it, our architecture has a better chance to succeed as a new piece of the city. Most cities have their temporal centers sometime in the past. I place Paris's temporal center in the early nineteenth century and New York's in the early twentieth century. Some cities, such as Los Angeles or Hong Kong, have their temporal centers in the future. They are perceived by their citizens as still being made and moving toward their fullness. These cities allow for quite different responses than those that see their ideal moment in the past. Cities can change their temporal center: Rome and London changed it more than once, but the forces that produce these changes are much greater than those of a few new buildings.

Design processes such as searching for the temporal center of a place have become useful only in this century, when the speed of change has become accelerated, when we build with new materials and systems,

65. Mont Saint-Michel,
Normandy, France,
thirteenth century

66. Temple of Kiomizu,
Kyoto, Japan, ninth
century

67. Machu Picchu,
Peru, c. 1500

Opposite
68. Reinhard &
Hofmeister, Corbett,
Harrison & MacMurray,
Raymond Hood, Godley
& Fouilhoux, Rockefeller
Center, New York, New
York, 1940

and when the dominant ideology of modernism impels us to break with the past. For architects of earlier times, fitting new buildings into their physical context was a natural part of their design.

When we first become architects, we are delighted to be given a piece of a city or a landscape to design—however small it may be. As we seek to create the best possible design, we face the sometimes conflicting goals of making the building relate to its place or to our favorite forms. I believe that cities and landscapes are more important than any building, and that the building is more important than the architect.

In architecture, each building has a role to play, expressing its particular nature and its place in the city or the landscape. It may be helpful to keep in mind that the best actors, the artists of acting, are those who enhance the whole cast and most completely express each particular role, surmounting their own personalities, rather than those who steal the show and always play themselves.

To design a building means to participate in the never-complete, collaborative work of art that is a city, perhaps the most important work of art any culture can produce. Cities are continually being remade. They grow and change through a large number of pragmatic and poetic answers to needs, but the cities we love also have encouraged some daring creative acts, such as the Chrysler Building and Central Park in New York, the Eiffel Tower in Paris, and the spires of the Sagrada Familia in Barcelona.

City design

Forces much greater than architecture are unraveling our cities. Probably the most damaging are rapid population growth and the passion for the private automobile. But our profession, with the best of intentions, has also contributed to the unraveling. Perhaps at the bottom of our ill-considered actions is the old conceit that designing a city is not very different from designing a house or a chair. Therefore, knowing how to design beautiful buildings qualifies a person to reshape our cities. Because Le Corbusier's stature as an architect was unmatched, it was easy for the profession to favorably receive his city design ideas. His concepts were endorsed by the Congrès International d'Architecture Moderne

(CIAM) at La Sarraz in 1928 and were later compiled in the Athens Charter of 1941. These proposals included slum clearance, separation of city functions by zones (housing, working, recreation, and circulation), placing housing in tall buildings surrounded by green spaces, and the formal design (not just the planning) of whole sections of cities. The Athens Charter even proposed that the state impose these designs on society. The planning ideas of CIAM were welcomed as offering the tools with which to make healthy, clean, efficient, and exciting new cities. Unfortunately, when these ideas were applied to real areas of the world, in many cases they did much damage.

In the 1950s, the city of New Haven, where I now live, was in the forefront of implementing some of these ideas, accompanied by idealism and widespread professional encouragement. Poor but viable neighborhoods were razed, against the expressed wishes of their inhabitants, and blocks of small houses and shops were replaced by an inessential expressway and public housing towers. Only a few miles of the expressway were built; the plans for its completion had to be abandoned because of strong public opposition. The razed neighborhoods and the expressway stub created a gulf in the city, still open today, and the housing towers became so unsafe that they had to be demolished years later. The results of these and other interventions compounded the already serious problems of this aging industrial city.

Schools, signatures, and cities

Recent cultural developments are also contributing to the loss of character of some cities. The old concepts of aesthetic schools and personal styles have been transformed by the ethos of our culture and the globalization of our practice. At least since the Renaissance, artists with shared ideals have grouped together to energize one another. And individual artists have preferred and mastered certain forms, which then have characterized their work. These natural developments gave a direction to the artistic search, and social norms assured that there would be only moderate stylistic differences between contemporaneous groups or individual artists. The old balance has been lost. Today, each school defines itself by a clearly recognizable aesthetic system that its followers apply to all circumstances. And individual preferences have evolved into highly differentiated personal styles from which architects rarely dare to depart. The effects of these exaggerations are compounded by the widespread nature of today's practices. The projects of almost every well-known architect range from houses to museums to whole city blocks, and from Shanghai to Frankfurt. A responsible architecture would guide all designs to fit into these different contexts with appropriately tailored architectural responses. This is very difficult to achieve if we consistently apply to every project the systems of forms of our artistic schools or our own signatures. If we continue to build variations of the same designs in every city of the world, these cities will lose their individuality and will become collections of passing fashions. Small traditional cities are even more vulnerable to losing their special character and risk becoming second-rate versions of larger cities. The center of Kyoto—that storehouse of architectural treasures, for example—is fast becoming a poor imitation of Osaka or Tokyo.

Foreground and background

Great cities have a fabric of well-designed but unexceptional buildings. These ensembles of buildings impress us with their aesthetic coherence. Great cities also have intelligent plans that organize buildings, spaces, and functions in agreeable ways and take the best advantage of the nature of their site. In addition, they often have some splendid, eye-catching buildings, usually with purposes or sizes that are exceptional. Sometimes we refer to the buildings that make the fabric as background and the exceptional ones as foreground.

The obvious conclusion from these observations is that we should design mostly good background buildings, because the majority of our commissions are for buildings of average size, with ordinary functions. However, the ideals of the profession create an almost irresistible urge to design foreground, attention-grabbing buildings no matter what their purpose, size, or location. We want our work published, and we know that modernity requires novelty for a work to be considered art. Originality at all costs may be a reasonable goal for other arts, but it does not suit archi-

tecture. When all buildings become "original" and "foreground," the result is cacophony. This happened at several of the international expositions, even though they were carefully planned and had many buildings designed by the best architects of the time.

Novelty is important when a building is first published. In the published photographs, novelty is exciting while issues of context or urban coherence seem almost irrelevant. With time, however, the publication is forgotten while the building remains on its site among its neighbors, contributing or detracting for years and years.

Perhaps the issue of foreground versus background buildings has been misunderstood. A background building does not have to be boring, or disappear among the surrounding structures. Designs that reinforce the existing fabric of buildings and are in tune with the building tradition of a city can also be good and even exceptional as architecture. Early in his career, Frank Lloyd Wright designed many buildings in and around Oak Park, where he lived. Most of these wonderful structures were very inno-

69. Frank Lloyd Wright, Winslow House, River Forest, Illinois, 1893

70. *Frank Lloyd Wright, Wright Home and Studio, Oak Park, Illinois, 1890*

71. *Frank Lloyd Wright, Fricke House, Oak Park, Illinois, 1901*

72. Frank Lloyd Wright, Beachy House, Oak Park, Illinois, 1908

vative, but they all fit appropriately into their surroundings and were appreciated as good neighbors by the community (figs. 69–72).

A building can be foreground and also in sympathy with the fabric of the city of which it is a part. This civility will not reduce, and actually may increase, the power of its architecture. Much of the strength and enduring appeal of the Monadnock Building derives from the fact that it looks like a Chicago building. It is an excellent version of the norm. Perhaps the best example of a foreground building in sympathy with the fabric of its city is Chartres Cathedral (fig. 73), one of the great buildings of all ages, and

73. Cathedral of Notre Dame, Chartres, France, twelfth century

exceptionally beautiful. It is made of the same gray stone as all the surrounding structures. The technology used in its construction was similar to that used in lesser buildings in the vicinity, only more sophisticated. When we approach Chartres and see it towering over the wheat fields, the cathedral and the town appear as one: one form, one entity. It is one of the highest architectural achievements.

Urban character

Character may be the most important aesthetic quality of a city or urban area. It is what makes background buildings transcend their modest roles. Character is provided by elements such as scale, materials, colors, compositional strategies, and the way buildings meet the sky, the ground, and other buildings. Most buildings in an area with a strong character share many of these approaches. Sometimes there is a consistent style but this is not essential for maintaining a given character. Most people (including architects) recognize and enjoy the character of their favorite places. One could conclude that the character of a city is an important quality that architects should regularly address in their work. Unfortunately, design character is not something for which contemporary architects strive because international modernism has not considered it a worthwhile goal. The consensus on this issue is changing, but, if we care about our cities, it is still up to each one of us to consider character in our designs.

Good buildings connect with other buildings that preceded them in the same general location. They also make it easy for future buildings to connect with them. Some buildings fit well and welcome newcomers. Others refuse to be incorporated into a larger composition. The first are civil and the latter are uncivil buildings. The skill of the architect seems to make little difference. Civility or lack of it can be exercised at any level of talent. The buildings on the boulevards of Paris or along the canals of Venice or on Commonwealth Avenue in Boston present only a few great designs and many ordinary but suitable designs. But almost all their buildings are very civil. They adjusted to the existing fabric and welcomed future buildings. They produced coherent and beautiful streets, which are more important than any single building.

Urban areas that we prize for their beauty and harmony are mostly made up of buildings that repeat, with variations and refinements, a few appropriate designs. Thoughtful imitation appears to have been an essential component of good city making throughout history. If we were to revive this process, we would need to reconsider some aspects of today's architecture. Among other changes, the best architects would need to provide sensible models to imitate; and the culture, especially the media, would need to support good imitative work.

Preservation

The arts have responded to the changes of the last two hundred years in various ways, but mainly by emphasizing newness and the break

74. McKim, Mead and White, Pennsylvania Station, New York, New York, 1910. Demolished 1964

with the past. This has created an internal contradiction for architecture. Breaking with the past has artistic and intellectual justifications, but buildings are not just art objects. They become integral parts of existing cities. Many "modern" buildings look alien and out of place in the context of traditional cities. It is often claimed that in the past cities have absorbed many changes in styles and that the discordant building represents only the latest style. Therefore, it should be accepted, because in time people will grow accustomed to it just as they did to previous styles. We know, or should know, that this is not true. A building that flaunts its newness makes a deliberate break with the traditions that have built our cities. It is, purposefully, an alien exception, and a city can tolerate only a few such structures. This is an unnecessary outcome because a building can be modern and still fit in a traditional environment if we conceive its forms and select its materials with the goal of making the new building an appropriate part of the greater whole.

The historic preservation movement was born and maintains its strength largely because so few new buildings fit well into their surroundings. Over the centuries, buildings were torn down and replaced by newer ones without any great sense of public loss. On the contrary, the proposed new building was usually assumed to be better built, more in tune with current tastes, and therefore welcomed. This is not the case today. To start with, we cannot erect new buildings with authentic historic forms, because the crafts that made them possible are now rare and unaffordable. When a handsome and well-built old building comes down it reduces the stock, because the replacement will not have similar physical qualities. The public has come to learn that the new, modern building that will replace the one torn down will most likely not befit its urban context, even if it is designed by a famous architect. We architects have much work to do to regain that lost trust. Historic preservation in America has its roots in the mid-nineteenth century, but the case that brought this issue to pub-

75. Louis Kahn, British Art Center, Yale University, New Haven, Connecticut, 1977

lic attention was the 1964 demolition of Pennsylvania Station in New York City (fig. 74). The station, built in 1910 following a design by McKim, Mead and White, was a majestic structure with generous public spaces that enhanced the city. It was replaced by an ill-fitting and mediocre building for Madison Square Garden.

No tricks or formulas are required to make a modern building fit appropriately and respectfully in a valued context. What is necessary is the intention to do so, the conviction that our responsibility to the place is greater than our allegiance to any aesthetic system. We do not have to imitate the forms of the past; our design can be modern, but it can use forms, proportions, colors, or materials that relate to the old with sympathy and sensitivity. Louis Kahn's British Art Center at Yale University (1977) is a good example (fig. 75). It is respectful of context—the university campus and the city of New Haven. It belongs completely to its place. At the same time, it is a beautiful and contemporary structure.

The value of preservation is sometimes exaggerated to protect worthless buildings, or impede good projects, and the archival mind-set of some preservation groups tends to ignore the fact that cities are not museums but living organisms. However, in its purpose and in its accomplishments, the preservation movement has been, and still is, one of the sanest and most valuable developments in urbanism and architecture in this century.

The American campus

New York, Chicago, and Los Angeles are great, dynamic places that I much enjoy. However, America has not produced a large, aesthetically harmonious city such as Paris or Barcelona, although today only the cores of those European cities remain great. Their suburbs are as incoherent as those in the United States. Perhaps it is more accurate to say that this century, which has built so much, has not fashioned any great large city. Americans have succeeded in one area of urban planning: the college campus. The urban designs of campuses are exceptional in their widespread high quality. There are many excellent campuses and several extraordinary ones. Thomas Jefferson's "academical village" for the University of Virginia

(1817–26) remains the paradigm of campus design and is perhaps the best work of architecture ever built in America (fig. 76).

There are several types of campus design, but all the successful ones share key characteristics. They are pedestrian villages, providing an appropriate environment for a community of scholars. On most good campuses, the landscaped open space is more important than the buildings. The primary formal role of the structures is to create handsome walls for well-proportioned outdoor spaces, and, therefore, most buildings are not sculptural objects. The exceptions are buildings that house the most honored functions and are placed in prominent places, such as the library at the University of Virginia. Most important for this discussion, on the best campuses the buildings have a coherent character, unique to each univer-

76. Thomas Jefferson,
University of Virginia,
Charlottesville,
Virginia, 1826

sity. The character of the architecture is perceived as a physical manifestation of the distinct nature of each institution, and it strengthens the bond among its members.

The campuses we most esteem were built in the nineteenth and the first half of the twentieth century. Few decent campuses were built after World War II, although the United States underwent a frenzy of campus building during this period. Even the additions to existing campuses were not kind to their fabric. Most new buildings were poorly designed, out of scale, and ill-placed, although sometimes the offending structure was an acclaimed modern building. The damage to the old campuses was done not only by architects. After World War II, many universities faced unexpected growth in the number of students and programs, and abandoned their commitment to their physical settings. Buildings were erected quickly and cheaply, urban design considerations were ignored, and much that was valuable (particularly the landscaped areas) was ill treated under the excuse of expediency. By the 1980s, the damage was obvious and a new awareness of the value of a good campus began to emerge. Noble old buildings are being renovated, and landscaping and the creation of new buildings are being entrusted to capable designers.

Architects trained in international modernism designed many campuses and campus buildings after World War II. Some of them, such as the Illinois Institute of Technology (IIT) by Mies van der Rohe (1941) and Scarborough College in Toronto by John Andrews (1963), are strong attempts to reinterpret campus design within the philosophy of international modernism. However, they do not measure up to the quality of the overall environment of earlier campuses, some designed by eclectic architects. Examples of these are Ralph Adams Cram's Rice University (1912), the "forty acres" of the University of Texas at Austin by Paul Cret (1933), McKim, Mead and White's Columbia University (1893), and Stanford University, by Frederick Law Olmsted with buildings by Shepley Rutan and Coolidge (1891). International modernist campuses are also not as successful as some campuses designed by inclusive modernists, such as Eliel Saarinen's Cranbrook Academy, built in the 1930s and 1940s. The conflicts between international modernism and the needs of a campus for such qualities as coherence, design character, and subordination of buildings to open spaces appear to be insoluble. If we want to design a successful campus we should study with care the characteristics of the many wonderful campuses built in America in the nineteenth and early twentieth centuries and try to reinterpret them to suit our time.

Colleges are discovering that selecting suitable architects for their new buildings is not a simple matter in today's architectural climate. Some colleges, with the best of intentions, have created a new problem by adopting the fad of collecting architects with strong signatures. One such building, on the proper site, can add sparkle and interest to a campus. Several such buildings, by different architects, will rob the campus of its special character. On practically all the campuses we love, the tone was set by a core group of buildings designed by one architect. These were followed by buildings designed by other architects but in close sympathy with the existing ones. Because campuses are special places, we need to approach the design of a new building in them with care and respect. More distinctly than in a city, the new building will become a part of a coherent and excellent composition. Campuses are compact and simplified cities. They have much to tell us about planning, architecture, landscape, and, above all, place.

In 1958, Eero Saarinen was commissioned to design two new residential colleges for Yale University, to be named after Samuel F. B. Morse and Ezra Stiles. They became the eleventh and twelfth colleges at Yale, the first to be built since the early 1930s, when the residential college system was developed. At the time I was working in Saarinen's office, and I became the project designer working under Eero Saarinen and Kevin Roche, leading a team of some five designers.

Residential colleges at Yale are four-story buildings, enclosing one or more courtyards, where some three hundred undergraduates live in single rooms or small suites of two to four students. Each college has its own dining hall, lounge, library, some basement recreational rooms, a few classrooms, and a house for the master of the college, who lives there with his or her family. Residential colleges are the heart of social life at Yale College, and the informal possibilities for learning they offer are considered almost as important as the courses taken by the students. Because undergraduates spend most of their four years at Yale in one college, these buildings are very important in creating a sense of place, as well as defining the physical identity of the university.

Across a street from the magnificent structure of John Russell Pope's Payne Whitney Gymnasium (1930) but behind a block of private shops, the site for the two new residential colleges was at some distance from the heart of Yale, where all the other colleges are located. Saarinen, an alumnus of the Yale School of Architecture's class of 1934, cared deeply for the institution and feared that the students might perceive the buildings as outside Yale, "in Siberia." The circumstances created a dilemma for him. On the one hand, he was an acclaimed and committed modern architect, and he knew that the profession and the culture expected a design that would advance the cause of modern architecture. It must be remembered that this was 1958, a time when international modern architecture, although unopposed, was still in a militant mode, asserting itself as the universal style. On the other hand, he believed that International Style buildings could not appropriately express the character of a residential college, or of Yale, and would disconnect themselves from the rest of the campus.

To complicate matters, Saarinen was working with a modest budget of twenty-two dollars per square foot. In order to understand his limits, he had a cost estimator calculate how much it would have cost in 1960 to build the Harkness Quadrangle (built in 1921 and designed by James Gamble Rogers, who remodeled it into Branford and Saybrook Colleges in 1933). The answer was one hundred dollars per square foot. This meant that Saarinen had no recourse to the materials, details, or crafts that contributed so much to the character of the Harkness Quadrangle, perhaps the most charming of the buildings that give Yale its physical character (fig. 77). He then engaged in an investigation of planning possibilities, new stone technologies, and formal devices. He hoped to design buildings that would be received as proper residential colleges belonging to Yale. He was keenly aware that in following this responsible path he risked the reproach of his peers, who frowned on any designs resembling a retreat from the forward march

of modernism. Even in his own office his design was questioned. I had my doubts about many aspects of the design, but I respected his intention and fortitude. Today I can see that the specific choices of forms and materials were secondary to his resolve to make the buildings fit successfully in their context.

In his design, Saarinen pursued several objectives. They were all dear to him and affected each other as they developed. One important goal was to create pleasant courtyards similar in size to those of the older Yale colleges. He saw the courtyards as the heart of college life. This goal was achieved with difficulty because the site was irregular and a bit too small to accommodate two colleges. He also believed it was his responsibility to respect the nearby gymnasium. At the same time, he

77. James Gamble Rogers, Harkness Quadrangle, Yale University, New Haven, Connecticut, 1921

worked to develop, beyond his given site, a pleasant pedestrian connection to the heart of the campus.

Although planning issues were uppermost in Saarinen's mind, he also worried about the colleges' character. He wanted them to be modern but also to be as charming and loved as the older colleges. This was difficult because he would not design in historical styles, which he considered false, and he did not have the budget for the richly crafted details common in older Yale buildings. His office explored contemporary construction systems and came up with a unique technology of walls of reinforced concrete with exposed large stones. These walls do not look like the older load-bearing walls of cut stone, but they were quite inexpensive, and they are stone.

We also thoroughly studied the students' rooms, building several full-scale brown-paper mock-ups to test their irregular shapes and built-in furniture. We worked with code officials to give the new colleges multiple entryways onto staircases, because, as older colleges showed, this arrangement enables the smaller social units that students like. Saarinen convinced Yale to engage Constantino Nivola and Oliver Andrews to create and place some forty-five sculptural pieces throughout the courtyards and other public spaces. These added considerable charm and richness to the students' environment.

Saarinen was asked to provide a single kitchen for the two dining halls. This was a difficult request because the colleges needed to appear independent and disconnected. He solved the problem by tucking the kitchen beneath a pedestrian walkway to the gym. This solution also enhanced the experience of going from the campus to the gym, providing a functional and conceptual connection between the new and old buildings.

In all these efforts, Saarinen continued to study carefully the qualities that made the old colleges at Yale such successful living and learning environments. He endeavored to re-create those qualities using a modern vocabulary. He did not start with the modern forms and then try to fit the functions in them. The buildings were finished within their budget in 1963 and have made their surrounding area much better by their presence. The Payne Whitney Gymnasium gained a large

forecourt, and Yale gained a new and "collegiate" pedestrian connector for the gym, colleges, and central campus. The gym building had never before looked so noble. The popularity of Stiles and Morse Colleges among students has gone up and down with the times, but they are perceived as completely Yale (fig. 78).

Eero Saarinen died in September 1961 when construction on the colleges had just begun. Even so, he did not escape the wrath of many architecture critics. It is difficult to forgive a person of influence who acts against principles that we cherish as faith but cannot justify logically. When the buildings were finished, not every critic disapproved, and some praised the appropriateness of Saarinen's design and his courage in going against a trend. Today, Stiles and Morse Colleges stand as very personal interpretations of modernity and of Yale's character. They are also important early examples of contemporary buildings designed with respect for the special character of a place.

78. Eero Saarinen, Stiles and Morse Colleges, Yale University, New Haven, Connecticut, 1963

PURPOSE

The external and internal appearance of an edifice should be illustrative of, and in accordance with, the purpose for which it is destined.

—A. W. N. Pugin, 1841

Purpose connects architecture with the reason for each building's existence. Buildings are built to satisfy perceived needs. Architecture happens when people require a setting for their activities or want to celebrate their achievements. Much of the power of some works of architecture, such as Rioan-ji in Kyoto and Teotihuacán in Mexico, derives from their spiritual or ceremonial purposes, sensitively expressed in architecture (figs. 79, 80). In this century, we found beauty in the blunt expression of utilitarian purposes, such as in that found in grain elevators and ocean liners (figs. 81, 82). International modernism adopted them as models for a new architecture.

Purpose is one of the basic connections that shape a building. The logic of purpose and construction works from the inside out. The responsibilities toward place and context work from the outside in. This is an ancient and healthy tug between the private and public aspects of architecture. How the pressures are resolved defines architects, cultures, and epochs.

Functions

A building usually has a main purpose. For example, a high school's purpose is to educate adolescents. Its many functions are classrooms, auditorium, gymnasium, administration spaces, stairs, and corridors. Functions often define a building's purpose and are a key aspect of this connection, but by this I do not mean to invoke functionalism. Expressing the basic purpose of a structure is an architectural response that we encounter in every culture. Functionalists believed that all buildings should be designed according to the determinants of their functions. This goal was pursued by many architects in the 1920s and 1930s. Functionalism was an experiment that had considerable influence on the architecture of this century. It has left a useful legacy of rational justification for the forms our buildings take, but it has not been seriously practiced by any important architect since the 1950s.

We architects are expected to properly accommodate the users' needs in our design and to make the total assemblage of functions work well. There are new building types, such as research laboratories and airports, that have exacting and complex functional requirements. Older building types, such as hospitals and courthouses, have become much more complex and precise in their demands. Apparently simple building types, such as office towers, require highly precise resolution of all functional and physical components. We want these buildings to be beautiful and wonderful, but we cannot make them so at the cost of frequently impaired functions. Clients, users, and society will not accept it.

In *Space, Time and Architecture* (1941), Sigfried Giedion writes that in the 1927 competition for the League of Nations building, the winning but disqualified scheme presented by Le Corbusier and Pierre Jeanneret should have been built because it was the scheme that had "the most complete and best-conceived solution to the needs" of the program. The final decision of the jury could be questioned because it was made on grounds other than appropriate resolution of functional needs. One of international modernism's arguments for its own legitimacy was the rational basis of its forms. This is a good argument because the quality of functional solutions can be tested empirically. It is what owners and users naturally do after a building is finished. However, for nonusers, these evaluations take time and require some effort. It is easier for those who are only observers not to go much beyond the formal aspects of the structure.

Opposite
79. Temple of Rioan-ji,
Kyoto, fifteenth century

80. Teotihuacán,
Mexico, fifth century

*81. Grain elevator
in Buenos Aires.
Illustration from
Le Corbusier's* Towards
a New Architecture

*82. Aquitania.
Illustration from
Le Corbusier's* Towards
a New Architecture

It is in the nature of architecture to produce art while responding to functional requirements, but in the last decades a gap has opened. The pragmatic requirements of buildings have grown in importance and complexity, and, at the same time, the responsibility for competently meeting these needs has been downplayed by many architecture teachers and writers. Inadequate responses to functional and other needs seem of no importance when a design is published or briefly visited, but are not forgotten by those who commissioned and use the building. And it is in the arena of the real world, more than in magazines and books, that reputations are built and the profession is judged.

Form and purpose

People expect buildings to look like what they are used for: a church should look like a church, a hospital should look like a hospital, a factory like a factory, a school like a school. We want our world to be intelligible. We commonly recognize the purpose of a building because we have learned a tradition of particular forms for the type, just as we learned to recognize the letters of the alphabet. When we read a handwritten message and encounter one or two letters shaped in an unusual and personal way, we can guess what they are by their placement within familiar letters and words. If the number of oddly shaped letters increases, we soon reach a point at which the whole text becomes unreadable. The same is true of buildings and cities. When we need to shelter new purposes that have no history of forms associated with them, our best option is to try to express their natures in our design, using forms that are easy to decode. Old purposes can also be given new forms if these forms are similarly appropriate and readable.

Because there is redundancy in our social codings, we can tolerate, and sometimes enjoy, an occasional breaking of the rules. Frank Lloyd Wright's 1959 Guggenheim Museum (fig. 83) did not look like a museum—it did not even function well as a museum—but it became an accepted and lauded building because of its powerful form and beautiful space. Designs that break the rules may succeed if they are exceptions. They need the fabric of normality to be understood.

83. Frank Lloyd Wright,
Guggenheim Museum,
New York, New York,
1959

The connection between a building's form and its purpose is almost as important as its connection with its place. Society does not long tolerate widespread disconnections. Early in the nineteenth century, critical segments of society started feeling that the then-dominant classical style did not appropriately represent their buildings' purposes. The first reaction gave rise to the Gothic revival (the earliest serious challenge to classicism) through the efforts of Augustus Welby Northmore Pugin and John Ruskin. Pugin wrote: "Greek temples are utterly inapplicable to the purposes of Christian churches . . . neither are they better adapted for domestic purposes." The perceived limits of the classical style also gave rise to various efforts to create a new architecture, with forms capable of expressing more fully the building purposes that the industrial and social revolutions had brought into being.

Since the Renaissance the forms of the pagan temple had been employed in Christian churches and in palaces and civic structures with great success and surprising public acceptance. Classical architecture's versatile vocabulary produced not only good buildings but also livable and coherent cities. The appropriateness of these ancient forms became less clear when society began expecting its new purposes, of which it was so proud, to be housed in structures that expressed their newness. For a growing number of people, factories, hospitals, and office buildings looked incongruous clad in the forms of Roman temples or Renaissance palaces. Some new purposes, such as the need to house the 1851 Great Exhibition of the Work of All Nations, could only be satisfied with new architectural forms.

Artistic purposes

Vernacular designers throughout history have been able to produce comfortable, appropriate, and often beautiful buildings simply by adapting well-known local models to the circumstances of the project. This approach was very successful, but it is not available to architects today. The world has changed; there are no commonly accepted models, and society expects something else from architects. Construction technology gives us little guidance. To do significant work, we need to give aesthetic and intellectual direction to each project with our artistic purposes. To produce even a modest and unassuming design we need an artistic purpose.

We architects know that for a design to transcend its basic nature and become art, more than beauty is required. The aesthetic resolution needs to reflect an intention. This intention may be only a desire to maintain stylistic consistency or to express the tenets of an artistic school, or it may reflect a higher purpose. The artistic purpose may respond to a religious vision, as in Gaudí's Sagrada Familia; the search for order, as in Mies van der Rohe's Toronto Dominion Center; the sublimation of the spirit of a site, as in Wright's Fallingwater; the direct expression of theories about housing, as in Le Corbusier's Unité d'Habitation; or, as is usually the case, a combination of diverse intentions. One of the intentions of most designers, for example, is to influence, to some degree, the direction of architecture. To be considered art, a building needs to move others with its aesthetic power. Most architects work very hard, although not always successfully, to have their building achieve this power and become art.

The artistic purposes of the architect need to somehow combine with the many purposes and functions of clients and users. Skillful architects manage to achieve their personal artistic goals while respecting the goals and needs of those for whom the building is being designed. This balance is simple to propose but difficult to achieve. The demands of critics and peers, on whose approval our fame and emotional well-being may depend, are often in conflict with the needs, hopes, and resources of our clients. Too many architects have learned that it is possible to charm, bully, or tire our clients into accepting designs that do not quite suit their purposes. This attitude may make it easier to produce "cutting-edge" designs, but it relies on a breach of trust and, in the long run, is damaging to architects and architecture.

Perhaps artistic purposes serve us best when they are based on principles and not on specific forms. If we disagree with our clients on matters of principle, we can withdraw from the project early enough—probably before we are selected—without misleading anyone. If our principles are not in conflict with the goals of the project, we can then proceed confidently to develop forms appropriate for the circumstances.

The number of artistic purposes is unlimited and their evaluation is subjective and affected by cultural trends. We judge each building with our mind, our memory, and our emotions. Sometimes architecture moves us as only great art can. These are the buildings that we continue to appreciate centuries after their original and basic purpose was fulfilled. However, an understanding of the original functional purpose is necessary to fully appreciate the building. Architecture is not sculpture and beautiful forms alone are not enough.

Very tall buildings, simply by being higher structures than their neighbors, acquire the ceremonial purpose of shaping a city's silhouette. When very tall office buildings accept this formal purpose, and respond successfully to it, helping to give identity to their place, they deserve to be called skyscrapers.

It is a privilege to be asked to design a very tall building and have the opportunity to make it a noble skyscraper. There is, however, a nagging

84. *William Van Alen, Chrysler Building, New York, New York, 1930*

question in the enterprise of defining a city against the sky with a structure that shelters only an accumulation of private functions. It has been argued that the goal would be clearer and in accord with traditional hierarchies if the tallest structures in a place had spiritual or civic purposes. On the other hand, places of work may be better symbols for our democratic, multicultural societies than towers that assert the preeminence of a particular religion or the power of the state. The artistic and social value of tall buildings may be a matter of discussion, but I, for one, remain grateful to William Van Alen for his gift, to all, of his Chrysler Building of 1930 (fig. 84). It was built for a private purpose, but Van Alen's and Walter Chrysler's vision made it a cherished public symbol.

A few years ago, Cesar Pelli & Associates won an architectural competition in Kuala Lumpur that gave us a unique opportunity to attempt

85. Cesar Pelli &
Associates, Petronas
Towers, Kuala Lumpur,
Malaysia, 1998

a design that reconsidered the representational qualities of the sky-scraper. For the Petronas Towers (fig. 85), which reached their maximum height of 452.6 meters in early 1996, we designed twin symmetrical sky-scrapers with distinctive forms and silhouettes. Each tower reaches the sky with an appropriate, ceremonial gesture, but, more important, the space between them also has a recognizable and memorable form. The center of the composition—the axis mundi—was transferred from the solid forms to the space they define. The space is free of functions and the onlooker can assign spiritual or civic roles to it. We strengthened this quality by connecting the towers with a pedestrian bridge, not originally required by the clients. The bridge and the inclined struts that support it at its center create a forty-story-high portal to the sky. In many cultures, detached portals, or gates, represent thresholds to a higher world. This quality is already evident in the portal in Kuala Lumpur (fig. 86).

*86. Cesar Pelli &
Associates, Petronas
Towers, Kuala Lumpur,
Malaysia, 1998. Portal*

*The Petronas Towers respond well to the complex functional pur-
poses defined by our clients, and they also respond appropriately to
their place in the sky. The symbolic purpose, however, now resides in the
space between them. When I was in my first year of architecture school
at the University of Tucumán, I was very impressed by a saying of Lao
Tse's: "The reality of a vase is not in its clay walls but in the space they
contain. The reality of a wheel is not in its spokes but in the space
between them." I read it in a Spanish translation of a lecture Frank
Lloyd Wright gave at the Chicago Art Institute in 1931. He paraphrased
an English version of the original Chinese. The acorn of truth survived
all the translations and remained within me for many years, still
potent, to help me give form to the Petronas Towers and have them
respond, in the space between them, to one of the highest purposes
entrusted to an architect.*

CULTURE
ARCHITECTURAL CULTURE

*What would I advise to a young man going into archi-
tecture? To forget the architectures of the world except as
something good in their time—to beware of architecture
schools—and to avoid getting into practice "half baked."*
—Frank Lloyd Wright, 1953

All artists are influenced by the cultural environment of their time
and place. The general culture is an amalgam of contributions from countless subcultures in our society. There is not one single, monolithic culture,
and there are no isolated individual contributors. It seems that we need to
be part of a not-too-large cultural group in order to contribute useful ideas
and have them accepted. The group in which I and other architects participate can be called the *architectural culture*.

We architects, as individuals, are exposed to all cultural currents and
our work can be stimulated by thoughts from everywhere, but the discipline of architecture is primarily affected by its own culture and, to a
lesser degree, by that of its sister arts. In this century, the influence of the
visual arts on architecture has had a profound effect on our profession.

To look at architecture through the connection with its own culture
is to look at our collective self. The architectural culture shapes us. It
attracts us to the profession, forms us during our schooling and apprenticeship, and continues to direct our progress with rewards and
reproaches. It writes and rewrites the rules that define the desired behavior for architects and the accepted forms, theories, and models for our
architecture. Many architects, in turn, try to modify the architectural culture in order to bring it closer to their ideals. This book is written with this

intention in mind. It is also one of the intentions of my designs.

The architectural culture, in many ways, behaves like an autonomous entity. There are many concepts—ideas, terms, models, myths, and idols—that circulate freely within the architectural culture, finding strong resonance with its members. Few of these concepts, however, are adopted by the general culture, despite the absence of distinct boundaries between it and that of architecture.

The architectural culture continually evolves in response to changing pressures from inside and outside itself. It is difficult to be a serious architect without following the events in the profession. We want to know what the best architects are doing and what our peers value. We follow the architectural discourse, because buildings are not the only things we design; every building represents a theory. Collectively, and through our buildings, we give shape to the architecture of our time. Certainly, there are occasions when we want to concentrate on our own private search for whatever we believe is important. But one of the reasons to pursue a private exploration is because we expect to come up with results: forms or ideas that will contribute to the discussion and perhaps affect the course of the architectural discipline.

Active centers of discourse in architecture seem to attract spotlights. The urge to be in the spotlight makes us prone to emulate the latest exciting expressions. But it is difficult to be original if we are always followers. We also know that if we ignore the spotlights, our work may be left in the dark, never connecting with the culture.

Today the architectural culture is global. There are approximately one million architects in the world, although the number of architects who actively participate in shaping our culture is considerably smaller. The architectural culture maintains standards and continuity, and occasionally supports specific causes through many local, national, and international institutions. These organizations promote preferred ideas and individual architects through awards, lectures, and publications. Some set criteria for membership and, on occasions, censure their members. These institutions are inherently conservative, because their role is to uphold agreed-upon standards. When they acclaim designs with unusual shapes it is because those shapes conform to sanctioned ideologies. Architecture, like most arts, accepts and encourages the new as long as it fits within endorsed intellectual frameworks, but it frowns on traditional or new approaches that do not conform to those frameworks.

Architectural historians, critics, and journalists are influential members of the culture. They interpret and evaluate ideas, designs, and architects, and try to give form to the architectural landscape. Serious and perceptive writings are vital to our understanding of architecture, because observers often see things that are not apparent to the doers. Many other people follow the architectural discourse. They read books and magazines on architecture, attend lectures, and occasionally participate as members of client groups or review boards. This informed public is essential to our health.

Education

Most of us enter the architectural culture through our schools. And for most architects, our greatest influence is usually our school. A good teacher can help us give purpose to our life in architecture, and the teachers of architecture, as a whole, have much influence on the direction that architecture takes. Teaching can be one of the most profoundly rewarding activities. Teaching is in itself an art and requires a special dedication. This is why those who teach well and are also good architects are rare and valuable.

Schools of architecture teach, but just as often they indoctrinate. Teaching means opening new doors of understanding and providing students with the tools to ask their own questions and reach their own conclusions. Indoctrination means trying to shape students to fit into the mold preferred by the instructor or the school, and having fixed answers to questions about architecture; indoctrination is easier. It is not difficult for students to tell one approach from the other. When we really teach, exposing our ideas to challenge, we all learn. I strongly prefer teaching over indoctrinating, but there are circumstances (academic subjects, historical moments) in which closely guided instruction and well-defined goals may be most productive.

An effective school of architecture will guide its students through four phases, not necessarily sequential. The first phase is usually the acquisition of specialized knowledge: technical and intellectual. This is necessary to understand architecture and its culture. Our profession is complex and changing; we acquire the basics in school, and through our practice, we give full body to our knowledge.

The second phase is the development of skills, in particular, design skills. This involves discovering our own talents, developing them under guidance, and beginning to shape the habits that will allow us to do the most with our abilities. In the school studio setting, for most of us, our enthusiasm for design blossoms, and we gain confidence in ourselves. A good school will allow several paths of development for students with different skills and inclinations.

The third phase is the immersion in the culture of the profession, its history, myths, heroes, anecdotes, jargon. This process of professional bonding is necessarily biased. It permits us, as we gain confidence in our talents, to decide if we want to belong to such a culture. If we do, we will share the points of reference that allow us to communicate with other members of the profession and to be accepted as one.

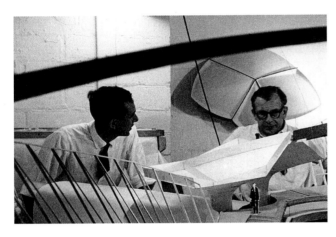

87. *Cesar Pelli with Eero Saarinen, Bloomfield Hills, Michigan, 1957*

The fourth phase is our own inner commitment to architecture. It comes about after we know enough to be captivated by the architectural culture and have discovered in ourselves a basic aptitude for the art or the profession. A moment comes, usually while at school but sometimes later, when we realize that we have made the decision to be architects and to abandon other possible futures. We resolve to dedicate ourselves to architecture. We hope to become very good architects and to be respected by those we have learned to admire. This moment shapes our career, and it can also shape our life. Inner commitment is an essential and strong root, a tap root.

Architecture schools

The world of architectural academia has grown enormously since World War II. It is now large enough to be a career in itself; it has its own market of ideas, independent of the profession. This is not altogether a bad development, because it encourages critical thinking, has created a large arena for theoretical discussion, and has led a number of good architects to become teachers. In many respects, the best schools of architecture (at least in the United States) are now better than ever. But in becoming self-sufficient, architectural academia lost the correcting influence of a close tie with the profession, and it has developed some bad habits. For example, students are often schooled in unrealistic design situations. Too many theories are taught and revered, not for their value to architects in their work but as mental exercises in themselves, and intellectual games of no consequence are labeled theories. Students are supposedly being prepared for practice, but they are usually led to think of themselves as independent designers, which is a rare condition in real life. This approach downplays teamwork and ignores essential, non-design roles in the profession. Most design teachers tend to be architects with very small offices, and often this is the only model of practice they teach. The larger, team-oriented form of practice is often poorly understood and sometimes denigrated, although it is now the dominant and most vital structure in the profession. This form of practice is itself rapidly growing, changing, and adapting to a new world of projects, technologies, and regulations. While universities are educational institutions and not training centers, their teaching would be more productive if their architecture schools presented more realistic images of the world of practice.

I offer criticisms of our educational process because it is vital to architecture. I love and respect architectural education, but it is my belief that it could do a better job of guiding future architects into the world. The practice is continuously being corrected by the reality of building. Architecture schools must correct themselves.

In a healthy architectural culture, academia and practice strengthen each other. Academia depends on the profession to understand the world of architecture as it really is and to learn from the innumerable experiments that architects carry out in their practice and their buildings. The profession relies on academia for critical thinking and for the development of an intellectual discipline to give rigor and direction to architecture.

Apprenticeship

Close in importance to our schooling in shaping us is our apprenticeship, the work we do with a mature architect whose work we respect once we have finished our studies. Schooling introduces us to the architectural culture; our apprenticeship prepares us to be full, contributing members. In our apprenticeship we experience, for the first time, architecture in its full range. We can share in the excitement of the firm competing and being selected for an important project, participate in giving form to the design and in the satisfaction of having it embraced by the client, and enjoy the completion of the building. The most basic new experience is that instead of working as individuals in competition with other students, as was the case in school, we now work cooperatively as members of a team. Others now depend on the quality and reliability of our work. As recent graduates we will not be able to take part in all aspects of architectural practice, but we can learn a great deal from other projects in the firm. Experienced individuals in the office can explain to us what is being done and why.

Architectural practice can be as much of a revelation as what we experienced in school. However, unlike the experience of school, where new insights are presented as such and seem to appear daily, in an office such revelations are not immediately apparent. They seep in slowly, project after project, in no structured order. We gain experience under guidance and by visiting and studying the built work, the result of all efforts. We can judge for ourselves what worked and what did not, and we can evaluate the ideas supporting the design. We learn from the projects in which we participate, and also from those of our colleagues. An essential lesson to be learned is how the sublime can be achieved by hard work, will, and a pinch of talent.

Architecture has become ever more complex and the mastery of its craft is not rapidly acquired. We shortchange ourselves when we open our offices shortly after leaving school. We may fail to learn critical aspects of the profession and the art. There are various ways to gain experience, but today none is as effective as learning within the context of a firm we respect. There, we can discover our specific strengths and develop them under counsel. In a well-run firm, we will be given increasing responsibilities, according to our capabilities, and will be able to assume important roles in diverse projects. In this manner, we acquire a record of performance that will later qualify us for similar projects with our own firms. This experience and its record have now become almost essential for starting a successful practice. We may never acquire it if we start our own firm when we are very young. The advice I give to most graduating architects is to work in a good firm for about ten years before attempting to work on one's own.

Writings

How architecture is described affects its development. The history of architecture, by what it chooses to commend, censure, or ignore, influences how we evaluate current work and what the culture considers desirable in our designs.

In recent times, most writings on architecture have tended to dwell on images and aesthetic theories. We have few rigorous analyses of built projects, particularly of those buildings whose design is based on a still influential theory. We are at a point in our historical sequence when much evidence has accumulated as to the validity, or weakness, of many contemporary postulates. If architecture were as disciplined as science, we would have examined and abandoned long ago many theories that, when adopted by the main body of architects, failed to produce better buildings and cities. We would have modified other theories in order to conform them to observed reality, and we would have formulated new ones based on the results of previous experiments. Architecture is not science, but we still can learn much from our collective experience. When the history of architecture allows us to learn from what we have done, from solid evidence, it is very useful history.

I grew up in Tucumán, a provincial city in northwest Argentina with good vernacular buildings but no tradition of architecture as a profession. I was first exposed to architecture as an artistic discipline in 1944 at the University of Tucumán, when I was seventeen years old; I fell in love with the subject while learning it. The university's school of architecture had at that time some sixty students and followed the structure and content of the Ecole des Beaux-Arts in Paris. I discovered that I could make beautiful drawings and washes as I was taught to do, but I won-dered what use my studies would have in my region of Argentina once I was out of school. Toward the end of my first year, some young architects arrived from Buenos Aires, fired up with the revelations of modernism, and changed the school. There were several good teachers in that group, and two stood out: Jorge Vivanco and Eduardo Sacriste. Later they were joined by another excellent architect and teacher, Ernesto Rogers.

With them, all of modern art flowed in like a fresh current, and I saw, for the first time, architecture as one of the great arts, capable of redefining itself. Instead of designing crypts and palaces as we had been doing, we started designing bus stations, hospitals, schools, and other equally necessary and understandable buildings. This was exhilarating. Suddenly, architecture ceased to exist as frozen rules and became a liv-ing art, with a social purpose that could fulfill me. The social and artis-tic purposes of architecture, as an art, continue to give direction to my work. There was tremendous energy in that school. Modernism was then new, still largely unbuilt, and full of promise. For us, in provincial Argentina, modernism was mainly about principles. We were going to design a new and better world.

The teaching of modernism at the University of Tucumán was, to a considerable degree, indoctrination—imparted with intelligence, excitement, and the good faith of the recently converted. It was not what most students there needed, and its impact on the city of Tucumán is questionable, but it was almost perfect for me. With several qualifica-tions, the school of architecture at the University of Tucumán was a bril-liant place for a short time. Within seven years, most of the good teach-ers had departed and the excitement had faded away.

I came to the United States in 1952 with a nine-month scholarship to the University of Illinois at Champaign-Urbana. My primary inten-tion was to experience America and its architecture. Fortunately, my design professor, Ambrose Richardson, also made my studies worth-while. He had recently left Skidmore, Owings & Merrill and was the per-fect guide to American practice and the American vision of architecture. He also steered me toward the office of Eero Saarinen and Associates in Bloomfield Hills, Michigan (fig. 87). During my apprenticeship with

Saarinen, I first understood fully what being an architect meant. I was for the first time involved in all the give and take, inspiration and perseverance, faith and wit that make architecture possible. My good schooling was valuable at Saarinen's, just as my experience with him was valuable later in my career. What, how, and from whom we learn in school and in our apprenticeship go far in shaping us as architects.

Eero Saarinen's office deserves further study. It cannot be a coincidence that so many important architects apprenticed with him, especially since his practice in the suburbs of Detroit was relatively small and lasted only twelve years. It would be useful to understand what made it an exceptional learning place. Perhaps it was his openness about the design process, or the lack of a mystique surrounding him, or the exploratory nature of each of his designs, but the fact is that Saarinen remains one of the least understood architects of his period, although he is still one of the most influential. Most of his important works were completed after his death and have never been collected in a monograph. Among the good architects who worked for him were Kevin Roche, Robert Venturi, Gunnar Birkerts, Paul Kennon, Anthony Lumsden, Edward "Chuck" Bassett, Wilhelm von Moltke, Nabuo Hozumi, and Warren Platner.

88. Cesar Pelli with designers, New Haven, Connecticut, 1992

My love for teaching is older than my love for architecture. I acquired this passion from my mother, who has dedicated her life to teaching and cannot conceive of a more important endeavor. I have always seen teaching as a duty and a pleasure. I started teaching architecture (as an assistant for a class in theory) when I was nineteen years old and in various ways have continued doing it all my life. I like to believe that my office is also a school, because part of the compact we architects have with the young people that come to work with us is to help them grow as architects (fig. 88). Because I enjoy teaching, my office is structured a little like a studio in an architecture school, and I often get as much pleasure from explaining a design intention as from the design itself.

CULTURE

THE ART WORLD

Our connection with the architectural culture is most basic. Our connection with other arts is indirect, but, in this century, it has deeply affected our practice and our designs. This circumstance, in particular the effect on us of painting's successful reinvention and revalorization of itself, requires special consideration.

Architecture was once called the "mother art." As recently as 1872, Eugène-Emanuel Viollet-le-Duc could write in *Entretiens sur l'architecture* "Sculpture and painting are to architecture what drama and poetry are to music, its derivatives, its necessary consequences." Such an utterance would be impossible today. Architecture continues to shelter most artistic activities, but all other arts have, for a long time now, been independent of architecture. The arts, their exceptionality, their number, and their individual characteristics, are not preordained by nature. They are cultural inventions. In our time, painting has reinvented itself, and this feat has had a great impact on architecture and other arts.

Architecture was perhaps the first visual art to recognize the changed nature of our time and to become modern. But the practice of architecture and the social role of buildings did not undergo a significant change parallel to painting. Many architects have envied the changed nature of painting and painters and have, in different ways, tried to emulate them.

My comments are addressed to an architectural culture that has been feeling perhaps overwhelmed by the intense presence of the art world. I have no criticism of painters or sculptors, from whom we have much to learn, if we keep in mind the differences between their art and ours.

The reinvention of painting

For some hundred years the most energetically independent of the visual arts has been painting. For centuries before, painting depicted the actions and appearances of the divine presence and its effect on human affairs. Saints and heroes, kings and bishops were all special agents of God, unlike ordinary human beings. They, their close associates, and their deeds deserved celebrating and recording, and the medium that did this was naturally exalted. During the Renaissance, an important shift took place. The artist gained status and became more important than the art produced. Sacred, heroic, and princely topics continued to legitimize painting as a high art, but the artist could choose other subjects that were also accepted as art. This was a critical change. Validation was originally given by the subject or the patron and later by the doer, the artist.

Starting in the late eighteenth century, the hierarchical, aristocratic-religious system that supported and legitimized painting slowly weakened, and, by World War I, it lost its exalted status. Also during the nineteenth century, with the invention of photography, painting lost its monopoly as the recorder of images. Painting was the most threatened of the arts, and its end, at least the end of easel painting, was predicted by some critical observers. Instead, painting reinvented itself as the magic lens that opens views to what would otherwise be invisible. Each painting became a door to new worlds of perceptions and understanding.

The reinvention of the meaning of painting probably began in the late nineteenth century, received great impetus from the work of several artists, most notably Cézanne, and was (for our purposes) rounded out by Picasso and Braque before World War I. This accomplishment, the high quality of the work produced, and the wide-ranging theoretical support that accompanied it gave painting a new and well-earned preeminence among the visual arts. Successful painters were compared to shamans and gained more authority than ever before.

The success of painting was aided by the portability of the art object, which could be sold, collected, and exhibited, adapting itself well to democratic capitalism. Painters, who in earlier times worked primarily on commission (as architects still do), now work on speculation, hoping for a future sale. The life of aspiring painters has become harsher and less predictable, but the strength and wealth of the network of museums, galleries, publications, writers, collectors, dealers, and artists have grown magnificently. This network is so strong that it has partly succeeded in appropriating the name *art* for painting and its close companions: sculpture, installations, photography; that is, for the art of museums (as should have been expected, some artists are now seeking to escape the physical boundaries of the museum). The network is often called the *art world*.

Their art and ours

The art world has been very good, with some qualifications, for painting and other visual arts. It has also been beneficial to architecture. However, it promotes concepts about the nature of art that do not quite suit architecture. Many of these concepts have been absorbed largely unquestioned by the architectural culture, where they remain undigested and affect the health of our profession. They should be reconsidered.

Artistic freedom. Such a condition may be an ideal for contemporary painters but it is a confusing goal for architects. A free architect is an unemployed architect.

Novelty and invention. These qualities are paramount in painting, in which each art object offers a new insight into art, life, or the world. This is their purpose and validity, the reason to paint a new painting. The purpose and validity of architecture are justified in other, more substantial ways. Invention is essential in architecture, as in all arts, but the unbounded pursuit of novelty in architecture, especially prescribed novelty, is damaging to our cities.

Aesthetic consistency. A painter pursues an inner vision in painting after painting. But aesthetic consistency is questionable for an architect whose projects exist for different purposes, in different climates, to suit different people, and to become a part of different physical settings. Consistent aesthetic development is also important when the life work of a painter is hung in an exhibition. The retrospective exhibition has become an important way to celebrate, and evaluate, a painter's life work. The buildings of an architect will never be displayed one next to the other, in a museum or anywhere else. They will remain, doing their job, where they were built. The art book, catalog, or monograph adds to the confusion. For the work of a painter, a book of pictures is a facsimile of an exhibition, of a real condition, and a photograph can reproduce the complete painting, however poorly. For an architect, the monograph is only a guide to the work: useful but distorted and incomplete—much like an illustrated guide to a city. A whole book of photographs cannot capture one percent of the many things a good building is. A monograph creates the false impression that the aesthetic relationship between the different buildings of an architect is important, while it downplays the truly important relationship between each building and its place. The consistency that matters is among the buildings of a city, not among the architect's scattered works.

Ownership. Paintings today belong to the painters, which was not the case in earlier times. That is why painters can sell their works and why only they have a say in the qualities of their paintings, even commissioned paintings. Architecture, in contrast, has many owners. The architect conceives it, but the legal owner is the client, who can sell it. The building also belongs to the people who use it, to the city or neighborhood of which it is part, and to its citizens. They all have a say in the qualities of the building because they all have to live with it. The legitimacy of historic preservation is based on this perception of widespread ownership rights.

Collections. Painting collections, unlike architectural collections, define the art of a period with its best examples. All other paintings, the great majority, can be ignored. Cities are our architectural collections, formed by the work of good, bad, and indifferent architects. They all matter.

Art. Finally, many architects and critics have accepted the idea that "art" is what painters and sculptors do, and that forms that resemble those of painting or sculpture are, therefore, more "art" than architectural forms. This comes from an unfounded sense of inferiority on the part of architecture. Architecture continues to be the richest, and the sturdiest, of the visual arts. If some of us wish to use forms derived from other arts, it is our right. But when we use such forms, their value comes not from the art in which they originated but from the architecture they help to make, evaluated as architecture.

Other arts

All types of artistic expression are equally important. They all can teach us something. The relationship between architecture and the performing arts is less direct than that between architecture and sculpture or painting. But the performing arts can also help us to understand ourselves better. As in architecture, in a play, opera, ballet, or film, a single person cannot do it all. Scores of people are necessary, to provide finances, direct the efforts, design stage sets and costumes, light the show, and perform in it. The final piece may be a work of art. It will certainly be the product of collaboration. In the performing arts, collaboration is even more essential and more intimate than it is in architecture. The composer of a musical work, for example, is not the only artist; the performers and the conductor are also critical and are artists as well. They interpret the work, rather than simply execute it. Each production of the same piece will be, to some degree, different. As is the case in architecture, the lack of a single control does not make a symphony less valuable as a work of art. The performing arts are deeply affected by their own culture (musical culture, theater culture, dance culture). But ultimately, like architecture (and unlike painting), they need to reach the large public or they will not thrive.

I have already expressed my concerns about contemporary architecture's disregard for the role a new building must play as part of its larger whole. A new building should make the urban context better by its addition to be called good architecture. The most beautiful description I know of the critical relationship of the parts to the whole is by Sor Juana Inez de la Cruz. The following is an excerpt from "Music" (c. 1680), one of her poems, translated by Diana Balmori:

No es otra cosa lo Hermoso
que una proporción que ordena
bien unas partes con otras:
pues no bastara ser bellas
absolutamente, si
relativa no lo fueran.
Destemplado un instrumento,
(aunque tenga la madera
más apta para el sonido;
aunque las más finas cuerdas
se le pongan; y en fin, aunque
en la forma y la materia
se apure el primor del Arte),
como sin concierto suena,
más que deleita, disgusta;
más que acaricia, atormenta.
Así la Beldad no está
sólo en que las partes sean
excesivamente hermosas,
sino en que unas a otras tengan
relativa proporción.

*Beauty
is nothing
but a proportion
that orders
one part
with another:
it's not enough
for each part
to be beautiful
if not beautiful
in their relation
to one another.
An instrument,
that is out of tune
though its wood
be sweet to sound
though good strings
on it be strung,...
will not be
in concert,
and will give pain
rather than pleasure.
Beauty
lies then
not in exceedingly
beautiful parts
but in the proportion
they keep
relative
to one another.*

Artistic collaborations

Artistic collaborations bring into sharp focus the similarities and differences among the arts. When we collaborate, we not only learn about the ideals and crafts of other artists, but we also learn much about our own art and ourselves. The close collaboration of architects with sculptors, painters, and decorative artists is ancient and universal. The frieze of the Parthenon, the paintings and carvings on the walls of Teotihuacán and Luxor, and the stained glass and sculptures at Chartres cathedral are all good examples. Such integration of the arts is rare today, although there is a growing interest in reviving this type of collaboration. Many believe that something valuable has been lost in the near-complete independence that now exists, and various programs have been created to

89. Joyce Kozloff,
Untitled, *National Airport, Washington, D.C., 1997*

reconnect the visual arts. This is a difficult enterprise under contemporary artistic ideologies. These programs place too many people between the architects and the collaborating artists and usually start on the wrong premise. They are often called "Art in Architecture." Unfortunately, this implies that architecture is not an art, forecloses the possibility of artistic exchange, and leads to sculptures simply being placed on or by buildings. Art can instead become part of a building, affecting its architecture and being affected by it.

Most painters and sculptors today think of their art as an independent entity, best seen in museums. A different mind-set is needed in order to conceive art as a part of a building. In a museum, paintings are exhibited as very special objects, separate from the viewers. Ever-present guards remind viewers not to touch them. This is necessary and sometimes desirable for many works of art. When art is incorporated in a building, however, the relationship between art and viewer is changed, offering artists another way to communicate with their audience. An image on a floor (in mosaic or terrazzo) becomes very accessible, physically and emotionally.

We can touch it and even step on it without diminishing it (figs. 89, 90). Art ceases to be remote and becomes part of life.

Fortunately, there are now many artists who believe that participation in a work of architecture is an important artistic enterprise. Architects will also have to adjust and open their process to the contributions of other artists. A serious collaboration always implies some risk. I believe the potential rewards more than justify it.

A sturdy art

The modern world cut painting loose from its traditional moorings. Painting risked irrelevance but gained a new freedom that was used to great advantage. Architecture never lost its mooring. It continues to be firmly rooted in reality. Ours is the sturdiest of the arts. We do not need to envy painters. We can enjoy their work and also take pleasure in the unparalleled richness that architecture offers us.

My first participation in an artistic collaboration took place while I was working for Eero Saarinen. It was with Constantino Nivola, who incorporated thirty-six sculptures in the buildings for Morse and Stiles Colleges at Yale. Saarinen saw sculpture as playing a role in his building similar to that of the best collegiate Gothic buildings at Yale, but he went further. Saarinen wanted elements that would enrich and intensify the architectural experience, mark special places, and help to modulate spaces, and he thought that Nivola's sculpture could do this. Saarinen and Nivola had many discussions on the type, placement, and material of the sculptures. We started integrating Nivola's sculptures into the building design, proposing places for them, and considering his suggestions. Nivola did not model the final maquettes for his pieces until the buildings were well under construction, and by then Saarinen had died. Kevin Roche had assumed the design leadership of the firm, and it was his responsibility to accept or reject the models proposed by Nivola. I worked with Nivola on the specifics of incorporating his work into the building. His pieces were sculpted in concrete while it was still semi-soft.

*Opposite
90. Sol Lewitt,* Black and White Bands in a Circle, *National Airport, Washington, D.C., 1997*

The largest pieces required a block of concrete some six by six feet at the base and some eight feet high. The concrete had a retardant that slowed the hardening process, which gave Nivola six to eight hours to finish the piece. As soon as the formwork was removed, Nivola went to work with shovel, trowel, and spatula, aided by one or two helpers. During the short available time, he worked feverishly, following the forms of a small

91. Constantino Nivola, Sculpture at Stiles and Morse Colleges, Yale University, New Haven, Connecticut, 1963

clay model. Some pieces were freestanding sculptures, others were inserted in the building walls, and still others were light fixtures. They all became part of the architecture and made it richer. I believe Saarinen would have been pleased with the results (fig. 91).

I have experienced several rewarding and successful collaborations in my own designs, beginning in 1970 with sculptor Jean Tinguely, who made an exciting piece, Chaos No. 1, for the Commons of Columbus (fig.

92. Jean Tinguely, Chaos No. 1, The Commons, Columbus, Indiana, 1973

Opposite
93. Al Held, Gravity's
Rainbow, *National
Airport, Washington,
D.C., 1997*

94. Frank Stella,
Hooloomooloo,
*National Airport,
Washington, D.C.,
1997*

92). Most recently, I have worked with thirty painters and sculptors for Washington, D.C.'s National Airport (figs. 89, 90, 93–96). In these cases, I adjusted my architecture to accept the other arts, and the painters and sculptors adjusted their art to mine. The pieces have become integral parts of the building and of the architecture. This is good practice—much better than simply placing a sculpture next to a building.

In my work with Siah Armajani, the teamwork went further. Our work together started with the North Plaza at Battery Park City, next to the World Financial Center (fig. 97). This was a slow and vital collaboration that also included the sculptor Scott Burton and the landscapers Paul Friedberg and Diana Balmori. Together we planned the whole plaza and designed its landscaped and paved areas, fountains, seats, fences, railings, and light fixtures. Armajani and I also designed together, and saw built, two enclosed pedestrian bridges in Minneapolis, one in 1989 over Marquette Avenue (fig. 98) and the other, some two years later, over Nicollet Mall. Most important was our collaboration on the (unrealized) design for the top of San Francisco's Yerba Buena Tower

Opposite
95. Jennifer Bartlett,
Homan-ji III, *National*
Airport, Washington,
D.C., 1997

96. Kent Bloomer,
Foliated Trellis,
National Airport,
Washington, D.C., 1997

97. Siah Armajani,
Scott Burton, Paul
Friedberg, Diana
Balmori, and Cesar
Pelli, North Plaza at
Battery Park City, New
York, New York, 1989

(fig. 99). In these cases, Armajani and I produced the pieces together in such a close working relationship that today we cannot tell who suggested or produced which part of the design.

This kind of intimate collaboration goes to the very heart of the creative process, shaking up and giving new life to areas of our psyche that we had endeavored to shield. Such an approach (today) requires special circumstances to succeed. The artists collaborating in this manner need to respect and like each other. They also have to be able to leave their egos aside, to be open to all suggestions, and to be ready to consider and develop them fairly, however unsound they may appear at first. This is the marrow of the collaboration—when the same element is seen through the lenses of two different artistic disciplines. What is wonderful for one may be incorrect for the other. This moment may force an artist to reconsider some cherished tenet. An intimate collaboration, when it works, is also the occasion for some of the most exciting moments in design.

*98. Siah Armajani
and Cesar Pelli,
Bridge over Marquette
Avenue, Minneapolis,
Minnesota, 1989*

*99. Siah Armajani
and Cesar Pelli, Yerba
Buena Tower top, San
Francisco, California,
1985. Model of unbuilt
project*

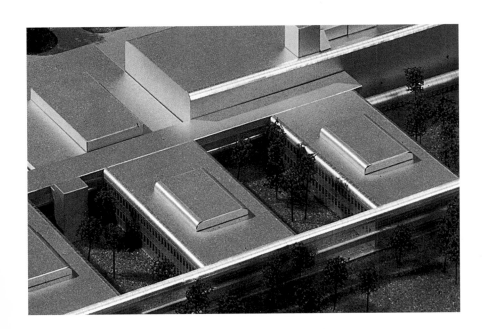

DESIGN PROCESS

*Architects who have acquired practical skills without
scholarship have never reached positions of authority,
while those who have relied only upon theories and
scholarship have obviously been hunting the shadow,
not the substance. But those who have a thorough
knowledge of both have attained their objective and
gained authority.*

—Marcus Vitruvius, c. 32 B.C.E.

All arts are intimately connected with their underlying crafts. The craft of the architect is design. It may be defined as the skills and knowledge necessary to conceive entire buildings and to prepare the instructions according to which somebody else will construct them.

We architects belong to a class of artists—which includes composers, playwrights, and some other visual artists—who do not execute their own creations. To practice our profession, we have to understand the craft of design; to be in full control of our art, we need to master it. We also need to learn to collaborate because architecture today is not produced by individuals but by teams. The processes with which we design affect our productivity, the enjoyment of our work, and the quality of our architecture.

Great architecture is not conceived in a single act—no matter what the stories say. It is developed over time in a succession of levels. We can carry the design upward, to one level after another, with graceful leaps or by climbing on our hands and knees. How we get there is not important. The goal is the same: the best architecture for the circumstances. With experience, we develop many ways of reaching our objective while satisfying schedules, budgets, and clients. We want every design to become wonderful architecture. But we are wise to recognize that there are limits and that not all projects have the same potential. Architecture is an art of the possible. If we are too focused on the ideal, we may miss the way to the best that the circumstances allow.

Teamwork

Architecture is a complex art. Any structure larger than a small house calls for more than one person to fully design it, and still more to build it. The *hero architect* does not exist (and perhaps never did), but is imagined as an individual who designs the building completely, makes all decisions, and expects to be treated with corresponding deference. Howard Roark, the hero of Ayn Rand's novel *The Fountainhead* (1943), is only an exaggeration of what continues to be a widespread image of the ideal architect.

Many architects, even some who head busy offices, still seem to believe that, for proper fulfillment, they should be hero architects, making all design decisions by themselves, needing only helpers to execute their vision. Probably this was never a good model. Today it is at odds with the reality of our practice. Playing the hero impairs the efficiency of firms, weakens the morale of collaborators, and lowers the quality of architecture. In today's world the hero is likely to remain forever frustrated.

International modernism has been a confusing model in this regard. Most of its founders behaved unabashedly like hero architects, refusing to acknowledge their many collaborators, while at the same time the modernist literature praised teamwork. And perhaps the possibilities of teamwork were misunderstood. The team prescribed by the Bauhaus was a group of designers with equal responsibilities making decisions in a collegial manner. If the masters' architecture had proved as universally suitable as they imagined, this kind of team might have been a good model. The collegial team was reasonably well suited to refine revered ideas, but an office with such a design approach would have a difficult time surviving today.

Architecture, practiced as an art, often requires that we go a long way following only our intuition. Situations in which several intuitions point to the same path toward a solution for every step of a problem are very rare. A modern design team is structured with complementary and mutually supportive roles. In most design offices, each project is developed by a team, led by a design team leader working under the direction of a principal designer who assumes full responsibility for the results. An efficient design team is a well-trained and well-chosen group of collaborators with defined responsibilities and authorities. A team in which all participants contribute and question is a source of ideas, refinements, and corrections. No individual architect can equal the richness of points of view, skills, and eyes that a well-directed team can bring to a project. However, a team without leadership may never produce art. Great design depends on leaps of imagination that go well beyond the intelligent solution of problems. With rare exceptions, only an individual can assume the risk those leaps represent and trust in their eventual resolution. How far the design goes depends on the principal designer's vision, but that same designer will achieve more and produce better buildings working with a good team.

Leadership requires some natural aptitude, but it is primarily developed in practice. The most useful experience is to have been a good team member oneself. Opportunities to exercise leadership and assume responsibilities are not difficult to find in an office because most projects require subleaders to assign design tasks, coordinate with associates and consultants, and develop parts of a large project.

In most design firms, there are individuals who, because of their talent and understanding, sometimes participate in intimate artistic collaborations with the principal designer. This was true of Kevin Roche in Eero Saarinen's firm. It is also true of my two current partners, Fred Clarke and Rafael Pelli, who are excellent designers, and of three or four other key designers in our firm. The main ingredient is trust; trust in the individuals' commitment to the particular artistic search, and trust in their architectural intelligence and sense of form. The collaboration will be more productive if one person remains responsible for the outcome and has the last word on any disagreement. This tends to assure that there will be no serious disagreements. The design depth of a firm depends on the number and quality of these collaborators.

Giving form

To produce great architecture it is necessary, at times, to surpass the apparent limits of a project and carry the design to unexpected, exhilarating heights. We usually can conceive serviceable design ideas when we need them, by purposeful thinking, and sometimes we can coax our minds into producing exciting new ideas, but they do not always come. To design good buildings we have to arrive at useful ideas; we have to know how to search for them and to recognize a valid idea (or its germ) when somebody else suggests it. Just as important, we must be ready to discard a wonderful idea when it does not fit into the overall concert of ideas and forms of the project at hand. We can then add it to our mental file for possible use in future projects.

There is a crucial moment in every design when the mass of information is first given architectural form. Because this is usually an emotionally charged moment, the reality of the process has been obscured by myths and legends. Observers may enjoy them, but we, the doers, cannot afford to be confused about this act because it affects the whole design sequence and the quality of the building. For the hero architect, and as students are often taught, giving form is a private act of inspiration. Sometimes, according to the legends, these visions came to the great architect in the course of travel, just after visiting the site, or even earlier. They were sketched on a napkin or on the back of an envelope, and these sketches were then given to draftspersons to develop.

These grand gestures must be wonderful for the ego of the architects, but as a process they have at least two serious flaws. One is that building forms that are conceived before all the pertinent data have been fully digested are bound not to address some important aspects of the project. By the time the deficiency becomes apparent, the architect and the client will have become attached to the forms, and then, most likely, great efforts will be made to modify the design while maintaining the inappropriate though pleasing image. If attempts at modification finally prove impossible, it may be necessary to redesign, disappointing everyone involved and endangering the project. The second flaw is that the team will be given a design already conceived in its main characteristics. A group of professionals will be disengaged from the process and thus denied a sense of responsibility. A distance will be created (perhaps purposely) that will not allow for early review and criticism from the team. This can only weaken the design, because a team is focused on a single project and understands the particulars of the problem much better than the principal architect, who is involved in several projects and has many other responsibilities toward the firm and its clients. And fame also can make great demands on the time of an architect.

Other ways to begin a design may be better suited to today's practice. My own approach is to try first to understand the characteristics of the project. Before I try to conceive a formal answer, I, with my partners and members of the team, become familiar with the site and its physical and cultural environment, the specific functions and purpose of the building, and relevant historical precedents. We have long meetings with users and clients to try to learn as clearly as possible the particulars of their hopes and needs. We prepare extensive photographic records and build scale models of the site, including its topography and surrounding structures. Members of my team visit city officials to clarify zoning and other regulations that may affect the project. At the same time, we start a systematic analysis of the program, confirm it with the users, and build block models of its elements to scale. Placing these blocks on the site model gives us an initial understanding of the impact of the required bulk on the given site and its environment. We prepare adjacency and flow diagrams, and, together with users of the future building, we make functional plans using simple methods, such as pasting together colored rectangles of the program elements. We continue until we have mastered the functional options of the problem and are able to propose optimal arrangements of the required elements, appropriate to the site.

There are several goals in this initial process. Our aim is to design a building well suited to its place and purpose and to come as close as possible to giving clients and users all that they expect in the building. The process allows us to avoid pursuing unsuitable schemes and gives us an early view of the whole landscape of design possibilities in which we can try to discern, before we start to design, the road that will allow the architecture to reach the highest level possible. We begin to consider architectural forms only after we possess a thorough understanding of the problem and of the range of possibilities it offers. Waiting to give form until after we have entered the world of the project and become attuned to its special qualities allows our design to flow naturally, as if from the inner nature of the problem.

No matter when architectural ideas may come to me, I always wait until I am with my team to sketch them. I draw them as diagrammatically as possible and try to explain the reasons and intentions for my designs. If I cannot put my intentions in words, this tells me that my ideas are not clear. For me, each project requires a backbone of ideas. Describing my intentions with drawings and words allows me to define the formal and theoretical intentions for the project. All the members of my team are free to propose alternative solutions, make suggestions, correct my assumptions, or question my goals. And they do. From the very beginning, the designers working with me are my collaborators. In our discussions, we try to expose and clarify any hidden or mysterious aspects of the design. Then all efforts can be intelligently focused on the architectural goals we have set.

Different building types call for different designs suited to their unique order of values. For example, aesthetics may be paramount in the design of a museum but secondary for public housing, where providing the maximum amount of usable space within the budget and creating a stable and secure neighborhood are more important. In the design of a hospital, efficient function and the patient's well-being come first. And for an infill building, appropriateness to the surroundings (in harmony or in contrast) may have the greatest weight. These varying hierarchies of values reach deep into the design, and we try to make them clear to ourselves as early on as possible.

The role of the architect is often seen as similar to that of a classical sculptor, who conceives a form and imposes it on a marble block. I see the role of the architect more like that of a gardener. The gardener understands the nature of a particular site, its climate, soil, shade, and nurtures each plant so that it can become the best possible example of its species. A gardener caring for an apple tree tries to make it grow into a healthy specimen covered with blossoms and fruits; a pine tree, however, is guided and pruned to achieve the most elegant form possible rather than bloom or bear fruit. Buildings, with their changing needs and their attachment to a site, are more like living trees than inert blocks of stone.

Alternatives

We have a better chance of satisfying the needs of users and clients if, at all design stages, we consider possible alternative solutions rather than concentrate on only one answer. Alternative design solutions are not superficial constructs. They usually grow naturally as we consider the still undefined priorities among the diverse goals of a project. As we reorder priorities, architectural responses change, sometimes dramatically. Discussion of priorities is one of the most useful interchanges of ideas that we have with clients and users. Obviously, it is wise to propose only design options that we support and feel confident can be developed into good architecture. Drawings and models of several alternatives allow clients to engage with the process and to participate in analyzing the designs. Clients' participation is more fruitful when each alternative design addresses all pertinent goals, not just aesthetic ones. Even when clients have little knowledge of architecture, they react intelligently if presented with easy-to-understand true options. When clients are shown a single design or only formal variations on the same idea, they may feel dissatisfied, but, not understanding that there might be other architectural answers to their needs, and perhaps intimidated by the architect's authority, they may be reluctant to express their uneasiness. Clients may assent to what is being proposed, only to conclude later in the process that the design really does not suit them. This is an unsatisfactory and unnecessary development. In my office we have found that clients are more ready to support our aesthetic goals when they see that we make every effort to respond to their needs with our design, and that our visions for the building do not diminish their own.

Pre-design

Escalating construction costs and ever more demanding functions have increased the importance of practical concerns for clients and users. This has led some firms, like ours, to propose, for most of our projects, that we add a pre-design phase to the process. During this phase we study the problem, before designing anything, and analyze schedule, site, and the three basic variables of size, quality, and cost. We do this together with our clients and also with a good cost estimator. If there is a discrepancy, as often happens, it means that the size of the building must shrink, reducing program elements; or that the physical quality (translated into dollars per square foot and compared to that of similar buildings) will be less than desired; or that the budget has to be increased. We have found that it is much easier for our clients to make these decisions before there is a scheme to defend or blame. After program, budget, and quality are adjusted and agreed on, the project can begin on a firm basis, with attainable objectives. Often, and before the project starts, there is a hidden mismatch between funds and expectations. This means that a reconciliation will have to take place sometime during the design process. Our clients usually can see that the earlier this problem is addressed, the easier it is to solve and the less damaging it is to the project.

Design decisions

In trying to understand the essence of the design process, I have come to believe that having clear objectives and making good decisions is probably more important than generating ideas or forms. Tens of thousands of ideas are considered for any project. Ideas are essential, but they are not hard to elicit. A good designer will come up with one idea after another when considering a design problem. Forms are more elusive, but, if we have the inclination and the training, they are not too difficult to conceive. The crucial act is discerning which ideas and forms have the best potential for architecture, under the circumstances of the specific project. Perhaps more important than being inspired is to have a well-defined course, and the judgment and perseverance to keep moving the design in this direction. This opinion is reinforced by the story the buildings themselves tell. When I study the architecture we have continued to admire through changes in fashion and ideology, buildings such as the Parthenon, Hagia Sophia, Notre Dame de Paris, and the University of Virginia, I read in them many inspired passages, but, above all, I am impressed by the obvious intelligence, mastery of craft, and clarity of purpose of their architects.

It can be useful to think of the design process as a helical path, like climbing a spiral staircase. At each turn we review most aspects of the project, each time coming closer to a resolution and with a greater degree of detail. Our design follows a circular pattern, but the decision sequence (on the axis of the helix) is linear. Early thoroughness is desirable in architecture because once we have made key decisions at one stage of the design process, it is very inefficient to reconsider them at a later stage. Going back and making basic changes in the design is demoralizing to collaborators and clients. Reconsidering early decisions should be reserved for major crises or extraordinary insights.

There are hundreds of steps in the design of a building, each one presenting many problems to solve. When the circumstances are leisurely, we solve these problems slowly. We hope that with time the best solution will become obvious, and sometimes it does. This process is enjoyable, but most designs have somewhat tight schedules. Fortunately, we have discovered (as have many others before us) that with enough concentration we can focus on the design problem and arrive at a solution in one afternoon that is as good as one that takes a month to evolve, with the great bonus that the team does not lose momentum. Actually, a prompt solution is exciting and often provokes a cascade of new ideas. This approach requires discipline and probably more thinking than is involved in waiting for the decisions to decant on their own. But we can prepare our minds and ponder architectural issues beforehand, all the time, so that when the occasion requires it, we can respond promptly and thoughtfully.

A story I was once told (whose origin I do not know) has remained with me because it makes vivid one aspect of the creative process. Centuries ago, the emperor of China wanted to have a new painting of a rooster. All his advisers concurred that the best painter was Li Shiu, who was then very old and living in a remote location in the mountains. Emissaries were sent to the artist and returned with the message that he would be honored to paint a rooster for the emperor if he could have two years in which to do it. The emperor was chagrined, but accepted. When two years had almost passed, emissaries were sent again, and this time they returned conveying Li Shiu's words that he was very sorry but he needed one more year. He also added that the painting was coming along very well. The emperor, not accustomed to being kept waiting, was quite upset with the delay and had to be mollified by his advisers, but he reluctantly accepted the extra year.

Eventually, word came from the mountains that the painting was finished, and, because Li Shiu was too old and feeble to travel, arrangements were made for the emperor to undertake the journey. This he did, with the appropriate train of courtiers and servants. After some time, the emperor reached the high valley where Li Shiu lived in a large and rambling house. The artist was properly introduced to the emperor, pleasantries were exchanged, and tea was drunk, with no painting in sight. The formalities would have gone on for much longer if the emperor had not demanded to see his painting. Li Shiu got up and from a shelf brought a scroll that he unrolled. It was blank, untouched; he took some brushes he had ready and in a short time painted a magnificent rooster, the most beautiful anyone had seen. The emperor was at first enchanted by the image, but soon reacted to what he perceived as disrespectful behavior and demanded to know why—if Li Shiu could create this magnificent image in a few minutes—he had the audacity to keep the emperor of China waiting for three years. Li Shiu asked the emperor to follow him, and throughout the house, on every wall of every room, were paintings of roosters—hundreds of them. They were the evidence of a focused and patient search.

The finished building

In the finished building, all our ideas and intentions become one entity. Plans, sections, and elevations; sketches, models, diagrams, and details; material samples and technical specifications all cease to matter. We now have a work of architecture, belonging to its place under the sun and the rain. Our designs are only approximations, and the completed building always contains some surprises for us. We find in it the inevitable variations in workmanship and in the color of natural materials. There is also the reality, now independent from the designer, of the building itself. When the building becomes real, it reorganizes priorities, making secondary certain relationships that we thought were primary and bringing into focus conditions of which we were only vaguely aware.

To design is to explore partly uncharted territory. Usually, we are guided by our knowledge, skills, and reliable ideas. But occasionally we march ahead following an impulse. This is perhaps why, in our built design, we sometimes encounter a wonderful quality that we do not quite remember planning. We can then try to re-create the process that produced that "lucky" result. What once just "happened" we can now achieve objectively. The process is ours to control. For painters, thought and result are often simultaneous, and happenstance is not readily differentiated from purpose; for some painters, such as Jackson Pollock, they were one. For architects, design and building are years apart. The wait can be agonizing, but it allows us to appraise the success of what we planned and also what we did not. The finished building can be our most important critic and teacher. It may be a work of art. It is also the test of many intentions. If we study it dispassionately, it has much to tell us.

The workplace

All architectural offices want projects to design and need to earn enough in fees to survive. Beyond these basic objectives, offices are shaped by a variety of personal goals, such as fame, wealth, social service, and self-fulfillment, combined in innumerable ways. These goals deeply affect the culture and direction of the offices. They also affect the architecture they produce.

An architectural graduate who hopes to become an acclaimed architect and needs to choose an office in which to work and learn should visit the offices of respected architects, observe the work environment, and talk with the young people working there. It is a warning if an office will not allow such a visit. A good firm is a place where the work is enjoyable and rewarding for everyone, not just the principals. It is important to remember that not all offices that produce celebrated designs are good learning environments. Respected design offices can be very different from one another, and the experience of working in them can be more different still. The choice of workplace should be a careful one, because the learning years in an office are as important as the years in school in shaping an architect's future—sometimes more so. And although a recent graduate may plan to stay there only a few months, the stay may last for many years.

The quality of an office as a working, learning, and producing environment is affected by its size. Good environments are found in firms in which the total number of people ranges from approximately 10 to 120. An office of fewer than 10 people can produce excellent work, but the building types undertaken and thus the learning opportunities will be limited. If this size is permanent, the lead architect will tend to control the design and process without giving much room to others to develop. If, however, small size appears to be only a temporary condition and the firm seems ready to start growing, such an office can be a great opportunity for a capable young architect. When a firm is expanding, new positions with increased responsibility open up. A firm of more than 120 people can also produce excellent work, usually through a subgroup, but at this size, the office can only be kept together by a shared and overriding profit goal. Very large firms are rarely guided by a common artistic purpose. A creative young architect could be lost in it. Only business reasons can lead an office to grow larger than 150 persons. We have found that a staff of about 70 to 90 people works best for our firm.

Associations

We architects have long associated with engineers and other consultants. Today we also associate with other architectural firms. There are advantages to this practice, and that is why our firm was designed specifically to collaborate with other architects and structured to function in a variety of modes that can respond to today's diverse and rapidly changing constellation of projects. For example, we might provide full services, or act as prime (or sub-) contractors in complex teams, or contract separately as design architects. In our most typical professional collaboration, the firm's role is to conceive and develop the design, including plan organization, building form, and all visible details. In contractual terms, we are primarily responsible for the pre-design, schematic design, and design development phases of the project. Our associates are primarily responsible, with our strong participation, for the remaining phases, construction documents and construction administration. Our associates are often based in the area where the project will be built and have a good understanding of the characteristics of the place and its people. At other times our associates have substantial experience in a particular building type. This system of associations allows us to assemble, for specific projects, a team of firms that together possesses greater depth and breadth than any single firm can have.

Designing a firm to work successfully in association requires more than adopting the right procedures. All members of the firm need to be trained to respond naturally and at every stage to the needs of the association. Working in association differs from working alone as a single firm. It requires a greater distribution of information and authority from the principals and more openness, promptness, reliability, and watchfulness from everyone.

There are two good reasons to work in association. One is the ability to respond well to the needs of a great range of projects. The other is the culture of the firm. Associating with other architects allows my firm to design large projects while maintaining an office of moderate size with a loose, creative, and high-energy environment. This type of environment does not mix well with the production of construction documents for large projects, which requires a structured and tightly controlled process within an orderly, well-supervised environment. In contrast, good design environments tend to be lightly supervised, with changing groups of people active at all hours of the day (and night) working in roomy, atelier-like surroundings with drawings and models piled up on all desks.

Many aspects of the design process described were developed by my partners and me to suit us, with our strengths and weaknesses, in the time and places we have worked. When we become responsible for our firms, we need to design the processes that will allow us to do our best work. We architects rarely take the trouble to consider what may be our most important design, the design of our practices.

When I went to Los Angeles to work at DMJM, it was necessary for me to rethink the process of design. I had to produce under circumstances so limited that my previous experience was of little help. DMJM was already then a major engineering concern that numbered some seven hundred people, but had only four designers in its architecture department. The few architectural projects at DMJM came from clients who were not much interested in design but had other priorities—low building costs, short schedules, and modest fees. Budgets for design were given to me as the total number of hours my team and I could spend on a project, and they were always tight. One of the most interesting design commissions I encountered there was for a laboratory building for Comsat in Clarksburgh, Maryland. The firm got the job because it promised that construction could begin five months after signing the contract, which Comsat had stipulated. I had one month to organize and shape this complex building before we would have to start on construction documents. In the past, DMJM would probably have developed some simple connected boxy buildings to meet the deadline. By making prompt decisions and taking advantage of much previous thinking on issues of growth and change, and on the aesthetic possibilities of lightweight exterior enclosures, I managed to design a scheme that responded well to Comsat's needs but went further. My team and I also developed a new prefabricated aluminum enclosure and gave some clear answers to problems of flexibility and growth for a building of this type (fig. 100). Because schedule was the overriding objective, my rather adventurous design was instantly approved. The building was finished in 1968, on time and within its budget.

I have sometimes thought that my years in Los Angeles, at DMJM and Gruen Associates, were training, like that of Olympic runners who practice by running in water on the beach. When they move to a good, firm track, they can run faster and better. The Los Angeles offices provided very good training for me. The conditions were difficult but not impossible. I realized I needed to reconsider the design process and to distinguish what really worked from the pleasant habits and traditions I shared with other architects. I ended up taking a liking to tough problems, and today, although I naturally prefer projects with generous budgets and artistic goals, I still enjoy, on occasion, trying to create a well-designed building within very demanding parameters. Such works are a good test of one's mettle as an architect.

Throughout much of my career, I believed that I would never have my own firm because I did not have family or school associations, and I certainly did not have the ability to obtain work from strangers. I concluded that if I wanted to design, I would have to do it through other firms, with principals capable of bringing in new commissions. This led me to DMJM and Gruen, where the arrangement worked reasonably well. I remain proud of the buildings I designed in those offices.

In 1976, I was offered the deanship of the School of Architecture at Yale University, which I accepted. I moved to New Haven, Connecticut, and started my new academic life. Shortly thereafter, and rather unexpectedly, I was selected to design the renovation and expansion of the

100. Cesar Pelli at DMJM, Comsat Headquarters and Laboratories, Clarksburgh, Maryland, 1968. Model

Museum of Modern Art in New York City (MoMA). I was then only beginning to be known as an architect. The Museum of Modern Art started with a list that included all the best-known architects in the world. As far as I know, I was chosen because of my record of successfully designing adventuresome buildings within a framework of tight budgets and difficult circumstances. The selection committee, made up of some twenty individuals, included the architects and museum trustees Philip Johnson, Gordon Bunshaft, and Wallace Harrison; the museum's director of architecture and design, Arthur Drexler; and Richard Weinstein, a professional adviser. The committee narrowed the list to three architects, interviewed each of us several times, visited all the buildings I had designed, and took several months in their selection process. The Pacific Design Center was probably the project that helped sway the decision in my favor. At the time, MoMA had little money, a very complicated project with maximum visibility, strong opposition to its plans, and the need for several public approvals for its air-rights tax-advantage development. I believe I served them well. The project passed through a gauntlet of approvals, answered all the museum's requirements, was built for less money per square foot than any major museum, and provided a suitable home for the institution.

The Museum of Modern Art project necessitated opening my own office. Cesar Pelli and Associates, founded in 1977, is located in New Haven, Connecticut, one block away from the Yale School of Architecture. This allowed me to combine two exciting and demanding jobs: designing and teaching. I was aided in starting my firm and designing the MoMA project by Fred Clarke and Diana Balmori, who later became my partners and helped give shape to my practice. Fred Clarke, in particular, has contributed much toward developing and sharpening many of the design processes I have described in this chapter.

I started my office when I was fifty years old. I did not have my own firm during my early, most inventive years, but the late start had some advantages. I knew by then that to feel complete as an architect I had to try to participate in as full a way as possible in giving physical form to our time. This meant accepting the risks and limitations of designing the whole range of projects society requires of me instead of concentrating on some favorite building types. I knew I wanted to practice in the critical center of architecture, where all problems, pragmatic and artistic, converge, although I was aware that today's culture imagines that the pragmatic and artistic aspects of architecture are irreconcilable. I also knew that the sensitive response to each problem was (and is) for me more important than the exquisite object. And I knew that I preferred to continue to explore rather than to refine my favorite forms. Also, by then I had had a great deal of experience in other firms, and I knew the office I wanted, to suit me, my goals, and my times as I interpreted them. I would not have been able to design my firm as effectively if I had done so much earlier in my career.

CONSTITUENCY

All artists have an audience in mind for their work. We want to please ourselves and we also want to please others, our constituency. The nature of our constituency and its effect on our work vary with the arts and the times. Our constituency evaluates and validates our work. I judge a building to be art when it gains my respect and admiration and touches my deepest chords. It is socially accepted as art when many share this opinion, and the opinion is affirmed by the accepted agencies: publications, critics, and awards. The architect's constituency, those for whom we design, is complex. Four segments can be distinguished: client, user, society, and the media.

Client

The reality of the client is often at odds with the idealized design process learned in school. In order to practice architecture, we need to understand what clients expect of us and of their roles in the design process. We have to learn how to work with clients in order to answer their needs and to have our designs accepted by them. This understanding is best gained through direct experience, but the general aspects of this relationship may be discussed.

101. Michelangelo,
Sistine Chapel ceiling,
The Vatican, Rome,
Italy, 1512

The client plays several important roles in the making of architecture. A project begins when a client decides to allocate funds to build a structure to fulfill a purpose. Major decisions that are routinely made by artists in other fields are made by the client before an architect is sought: where, when, how large, and for what purpose to build. In earlier times most artists also worked under similar conditions. Until the Renaissance, the client determined whether paintings were necessary, what they would depict (the Stations of the Cross in a church, for example), where they would be placed, and how large they would be. Sometimes the client even prescribed the palette of colors and compositional strategies. During the Renaissance, painters began to make several of these decisions themselves, but they continued to work for clients, who often specified the subject matter, size, and location of the paintings. For instance, Michelangelo was commissioned by Julius II to paint the ceiling of the Sistine Chapel with scenes from the Bible (fig. 101). Other artists were paid to paint the walls. It is important for architects (for whom this interdependency remains very much alive) to keep in mind that the art produced by painters working under these constraints was of no lesser quality than the art produced by painters today. One could make the opposite case and argue that the discipline was not bad for the art and that perhaps the overall quality of paintings (produced by great, ordinary, and weak painters) in the Middle Ages or the Renaissance was higher than the overall quality of paintings made today.

It is worthwhile to consider the art of Velázquez. He was commissioned to paint portrait after portrait of his "client," King Felipe IV of Spain,

102. Diego Velázquez, Felipe IV, *1635*

and of his family (fig. 102). This family was not endowed with handsome or interesting faces, and Velázquez had to paint them truthfully, while making them look as good as possible, with no room for rebellion or irony. When I look at these paintings, they are fully satisfying as art. Velázquez's task was similar to that of the architect: to fashion the requested product and make it art.

Being selected for a new building is important for all practicing architects and a key hurdle for young architects. Clients sometimes establish a personal relationship with an architect they trust, or they do not deem their future building important enough to bother selecting the most appropriate architect for the project. But when clients care about their buildings, they usually select architects on reasonable grounds. In those cases, they often start by considering many suitable candidates. Guided by pragmatic concerns and talks with previous clients, they select three to five architects to be interviewed. Through proposals and interviews, clients try to learn as much as possible about the architects being considered. How handsome and appropriate are the previous buildings they designed? How satisfied are the users? How well did the architects perform their services? Did they design within budget and on schedule? How easy were they to get along with? The relative weight that clients give to each factor (and how well they assess them) varies greatly from project to project, and from client to client.

The process of selecting an architect has been shifting from a reliance on personal channels of family or friendship to a preference for a verifiable record of accomplishments in comparable projects. For young architects, an important part of their record is the work they did during their apprenticeship. Unquestionably, personality and empathy will always play a role in the selection of individuals to perform a personal service requiring so great a degree of trust as the design of a building.

Most practitioners understand how clients arrive at the decision of which architect to select, and the large firms with marketing departments have become particularly adept at adjusting to the many variables of the selection process. But young architects starting their own firms can be misinformed. Commissioning a building is a major decision for most people, and, naturally, they want evidence that the project will be in capable and reliable hands. Being published and receiving awards counts, but not as much as having a record of good buildings and satisfied users and clients.

After an architect is selected and takes the reins of the project, the relationship with the client remains critical. First and most obvious is the contractual agreement. The contract's main purpose is to define the services that will be rendered and the fee that will be paid for them. Some architects have claimed that architecture is an autonomous art and not a service profession, but whenever we sign a contract, it is to provide services.

Clients provide the program describing the constituting elements and the functional needs of the project. Throughout the design process clients remain as active interpreters and modifiers of the program and other project goals. We, as architects, propose architectural solutions for the clients to approve. We may be certain that our design is a masterpiece, but if our clients are not satisfied with our work, they have the ultimate power, which is to reject the whole proposal and end the project. Clients appear on the scene before the architects do and remain with the project after we have gone and are no longer able to affect its design. At that moment, the clients become the owners, and they can remodel or demolish the building.

Contemporary clients do not have the power over the person of the architect that kings and popes once did, but they have more reasons to follow the development of their projects closely. Architecture today does not limit itself to civic or religious buildings, structures with strong symbolic and artistic purposes but simple pragmatic requirements. Instead, it has embraced the whole gamut of utilitarian structures. These buildings require more involvement from clients, who have legitimate concerns about function, cost, and schedule. According to an old saying, an architect needs a good client to end up with a good building. A "good client" used to mean a supportive patron, one who would approve all proposals and agree on whatever direction the architect wanted to give the design. Such patrons are now very rare. Good clients are needed more than ever, but today that means people who care about the building and the art; are involved through the whole design process; are explicit in their needs and goals, likes and dislikes; and make clear and timely decisions. We can learn much from our clients and depend on them to keep us on track as we move toward the most appropriate, functional, and exciting buildings for their needs.

Clients decide how much money can be spent on the project. The effects of money on architecture are significant and pervasive. Money affects the quality of the building and the size and location of its site. Clients have strong opinions on how their money should be spent. This requires a close collaboration because the architect, through the design, determines how the monies are actually spent. Sometimes clients increase the budget, to allow for better materials or costlier forms, but usually the budget has little elasticity. The intelligent use of available monies has become a critical design skill, one that is rarely taught. We need to learn it through experience and, if possible, under expert guidance. Designing to get the most architecture from a limited budget begins with the earliest conception of schemes. Some building schemes are inherently costly, and late "value engineering" (changes to the design to reduce the cost of the building) may only destroy other important qualities. Other schemes are inherently economical and flexible and can be kept within budget while achieving various goals. Only the good sense and experience of the lead designer can detect, very early in the process, which path will take the design furthest while keeping it within budget. No external cost-control process can replace the judgment of the person who gives form to the project. Money does not have the poetic impact that place has on architecture. But designing to achieve the most architecture for the available monies requires as much care and sensitivity as designing a building to make the most of its site.

Users

The user is the lifeblood of architecture, and buildings are made to house users' needs. Design takes form around these needs, which define the purpose and detailed functions of a building. In our design, we architects try to respond not only to the functional requirements but also to the hopes and ideals of all users: those who will visit, work, and live in the finished building. Users are perhaps our most important constituency.

Sometimes functional diagrams are the best tools with which to think a problem through and to explain our ideas to others. A good functional diagram is a graphic synthesis of a theory on how to organize a building to best provide for the needs of users. Some buildings seem to be direct expressions of functional diagrams. Such cases reveal with unusual clarity the thought process and system of values of the architects. Louis Kahn's A. N. Richards Laboratories in Philadelphia and Le Corbusier's Unité d'Habitation in Marseilles are useful examples. In those buildings we appreciate the beauty of the design, and, with a little effort, we can also judge the soundness of the theory.

The final success of a building depends greatly on how well we provide for its users. How well does it answer their functional needs? How pleasant and comfortable is it to work there? How exciting is it to move through its spaces? Because these goals are important, we need to work closely with users during the design process and listen carefully to all their concerns. When the building is finished, those who will use it should feel that it is theirs and be proud of it and their contribution to the design. Schools of architecture, correctly, take users as a primary responsibility in design exercises, and most architects are well prepared to understand and respond to the needs of users.

Society—the public

The general public is an indeterminate and nameless audience, but a very important one. Most people may never enter the building we design, but the new structure can change their experience of the city in positive or negative ways. The public is always present in our considerations, and we should try to respond to people's views and hopes in our designs.

When we design, there is often a tension between public and private needs. For many architects, including myself, public concerns are more important than private ones, and we try to have the private aspects of our designs defer to the public ones. Accepting this position has several consequences. For example, in the design of a private building on an urban street, important public aspects of the building are its character, facade, and silhouette. They contribute to the form and character of the whole street. We believe that these aspects are usually more important than private ones: interior organization, expression of structural or functional systems, or allegiance to an aesthetic school. This conclusion will not satisfy everyone trained in international modernism. But if we give due weight to aesthetic and ethical concerns for our cities, we will probably conclude that suitable exterior form is usually more important than interior order.

Giving precedence to public concerns may also lead us to conclude that if a building is tall enough to affect the skyline of a city or town, its design acquires the responsibility of defining a public, recognizable silhouette that can serve to mark and celebrate a place. We find that when it is placed against the sky—notwithstanding the hallowed example of the Seagram Building—architecture needs to acknowledge that it has entered a special realm, dear to all and sacred to many. Most people sense that entering the sky requires a proper ceremonial gesture—and they expect it. This may be why the Chrysler Building appears in countless polls as one of the most loved buildings in Manhattan, even though architects can easily find flaws in its design.

Society is the ultimate recipient of all buildings. Owners will change and architects will be forgotten, as will all mentions of the designs in books and magazines, but the buildings will still stand, casting shadows, using fuel, giving form to a street, and providing pleasure or irritation to innumerable people over generations. Citizens have the right to expect that every new building will contribute to a better city and a more humane world.

Societies have learned that building is not a purely private action and have created many controls to ensure that minimum standards are met. Schools need to conform to national standards in order to be accredited; architects must register with the state after fulfilling complex requirements; designs must comply with federal, state, and local laws, and must be interpreted and approved by diverse agencies before they can become buildings. Some of these controls are essential, others are sometimes useful, and too many others are unnecessary and create obstacles to good architecture.

The media

There is another important audience with which architects want to connect: those who may never see the building except through photographs. This has become our largest audience, with a growing effect on our work. Sometimes our buildings are in the midst of major, well-visited cities and can be readily seen and experienced by those whose opinions we value. Often they are not easily accessible, and we depend on the publication of our designs to reach a wide public. We want our work seen as soon as possible to show off our new creation, and we also want it to quickly enter the discourse on the future of architecture. The main vehicle for the diffusion of our work, and the arena in which our ideas vie for ascendancy, is the reproduced image supported by words.

The contributions of the media are most important. There is, however, a problem: architecture does not lend itself well to reproduction and diffusion. In the process, essential qualities are distorted or lost. It is a common experience to visit a building that we think we know well, because it has been frequently published and discussed, and to discover that the actual building is quite different from what we expected.

It is useful to remember that essential aspects of architecture, such as the feeling of enveloping walls, the soaring of great voids, the changing light and sound that modify our sense of space, or the feeling of unease or comfort a room provokes, are not captured in photographs. We may also keep in mind that photographs leave out the kinetic nature of architecture, the time necessary to move around it or into it, and the changes in the building produced by our movement. We experience the reality of a building as an interaction of our immediate perceptions with thoughts and memories. When we enter the nave of a church, our impression of the space is primarily formed by what we see and feel in it. But this perception is inseparable from our fresh memories of seeing the church spire from a distance, approaching the building, seeing the facade, and passing through the entrance. Our religious beliefs and memories of earlier visits to the same building or to other churches also affect our perception. They are all part of the architectural experience. Some photogenic buildings leave us cold when we visit them because the experience of being in them is not sufficiently rewarding.

Published photographs are usually carefully selected views that leave out ugly or unresolved parts of the design. Sometimes we discover that a well-known building has, in reality, only one good side. Photographs chosen for publication generally omit awkward relations of a building to its surroundings, and each image can be substantially altered in a variety of ways. Even when unretouched photographs of the building in its context are included, they fail to communicate critical aspects of how the building relates to its environs. The success or failure of these critical relations is apparent to anyone who spends five minutes walking around the site. Because we want to keep on being informed, we have to try to compensate, in our minds, for the limitations of the media. Here, as in other cases where we must rely on the opinions of others, a good dose of skepticism will prove invaluable.

I see my buildings as pieces of cities, and, in my designs, I try to make them into responsible and contributing citizens. I am particularly interested in the public role that all buildings play. I believe that we architects should try to go beyond our basic obligations to the public, and our opportunities to do so are many. In several cases, I have proposed to my clients that they build large "public rooms" although no such element existed in the program. On four occasions, to my delight, the clients agreed. Three of these "rooms" were built, and a fourth is under construction.

A public room is a space large enough for several hundred people to assemble freely and easily. It is accessible to all, at all active hours. It should be welcoming and comfortable for very large groups as well as for a few individuals. It should have generous dimensions, with an abundance of natural light and places for people to sit and meet. The room should, informally and easily, accommodate public gatherings and performances.

The functional and social model for these rooms is the Italian piazza. Just like a good piazza, a public room needs, on its perimeter, cafés, restaurants, and a few shops to contribute to the life of the place. These facilities may give a public room some superficial similarities

with the central space in a shopping mall, but its purpose and character are most different, almost opposed. A public room is, in all aspects, for the public, and it belongs in the city center, not in the suburbs. Shops and cafés provide a contributing but secondary activity that defers, in many ways, to public needs. A room built and sometimes run by private entities is not as public as a piazza or a park. On the other hand, one can make plans for using it in advance, because it is an interior space that functions in all weathers. And because an entity is responsible for its operation, with explicit commitments to public bodies, it is better maintained and programmed than a truly public space. On the continuum from public to private, I place a public room halfway between a park and a theater. All contribute toward enriching the life of the cities in which they are located.

The first public room I designed was for the main shopping street of Columbus, Indiana (1973). It was named The Commons in a public contest and was donated to the town by my clients, Mr. and Mrs. Irwin Miller and Mrs. Clementine Miller Tangeman (fig. 103). The second, the

103. Cesar Pelli at Gruen Associates, The Commons, Columbus, Indiana, 1973

*104. Cesar Pelli &
Associates,
Wintergarden at World
Financial Center, New
York, New York, 1988*

*Opposite
105. Cesar Pelli &
Associates, Founders
Hall, Charlotte, North
Carolina, 1992*

*106. Cesar Pelli &
Associates, Chubu
Cultural Center,
Kurayoshi, Tottori
prefecture, Japan,
2000. Model*

Wintergarden (1988), is part of the World Financial Center in Manhattan (fig. 104). It was named and paid for by Olympia & York. The third, Founders Hall (1992), is at the crossing of the two major streets (Tryon and Trade) in the center of Charlotte, North Carolina (fig. 105). It was named, paid for, and is run by NationsBank (now BankAmerica Corp.). These three public rooms are in cities of very different size and character. Columbus is a midwestern town with a population of thirty thousand and is well known for its great collection of buildings designed by some of today's best architects. Charlotte is a fast-growing city in the "New South" whose downtown used to empty out at 5:30 P.M. The World Financial Center is located in Battery Park City, on the Hudson River at the southern tip of Manhattan next to the Wall Street area and close to one of the city's major subway hubs. Each public room was designed to respond to the specific characteristics of its place and to the people it would serve. We have proposed a fourth public room as part of the Chubu Cultural Center in Kurayoshi, Tottori prefecture, Japan; it is due to open in the year 2000 (fig. 106).

The three public rooms I have designed and seen built are very successful. They have been used and enjoyed by hundreds of thousands of people. Each one appears to have created a social focus where one was needed but none existed. In all three cases, my clients were happy to be able to provide such spaces for their cities, and they remain very proud of their contributions.

ONESELF

*Socrates: Now of all acts the most complete is that
of constructing. A work demands love, meditation,
obedience to your finest thoughts, the invention
of laws by your soul, and many other things that
it draws miraculously from your own self, which
did not suspect that it possessed them.*

—Paul Valéry, 1927

It is ourselves above all that we want to please with what we do, and
we are, or should be, our own most demanding critics. It is within ourselves that the wellsprings of our art reside, and they need caring for if we
want them to flow abundantly and for long. It is within ourselves that we
look for a compass to guide us every time we need to make a substantive
decision.

In any worthwhile activity we see what we do with two different
sets of eyes. In the midst of doing we give all of ourselves to our labors in
constructive sympathy. We are one with our work. A moment later, we
look again at what we have done and judge it as if from outside ourselves,
with as critical and detached a manner as we can muster. We redesign
again and again, trying to satisfy our inner demands, though in architecture time is limited and we can rarely please ourselves fully.

Ourselves and others

Actions that affect others have an ethical component. We architects
cannot escape moral considerations in our actions because we depend on
others to bring our buildings into being, and the buildings we design have
a large and lasting effect on many people.

Almost every decision an architect makes has two aspects. One is reflected in the question "Is it correct?"—does it satisfy the expectations of the architectural culture? The other can be summed up by the question "Is it right?"—is this helping or harming others: people, landscape, urban surroundings? These questions help us to judge any building, but their primary value is as guides for our own work. When we design, it is relatively easy to recognize the "correct" options. Teachers, books, and magazines constantly define them for us. But we have to seek the "right" direction for ourselves, using our own internal compass. The path our design finally takes is shaped by the value we assign to all competing demands. The resulting balance will be different for each architect and each circumstance.

The art of architecture requires innumerable minor compromises. It is not possible to optimize every aspect of the future building, and throughout the design process we make trade-offs. Worthy goals such as beauty, function, and cost are often in conflict with one another. Compromise is inevitable, but if we are clear in our beliefs and know what is really important in each project, we can be open-minded and generous with many aspects of the design, satisfying our constituency and respecting public needs while maintaining our integrity and the backbone of our architecture.

Stylistic consistency

When we start working as independent or lead designers, we work very hard on every design that comes to us. We are anxious to show off our skills. Our first efforts may be adventurous or may be refinements of accepted ideas and forms. At some moment, we discover that we enjoy certain forms more than others, or that it is easier and more natural for us to design in a particular manner, or that some of our designs have been especially well received by the architectural culture. These factors will tend to set us on a defined stylistic course. If our names are starting to be recognized, we may try to reinforce our identity by accentuating the characteristics that differentiate our designs from those of other architects. We are normally guided in this quest by how our culture and our constituency respond to our work.

When we start to develop our own "style," talent and luck may gain us a reputation that brings us new and varied work. Later, some of us may find that, if we take our responsibilities to cities and to the purposes of our buildings seriously, it is difficult to continue to apply the same aesthetic approach to all projects. This is a quandary. At that moment in our careers, we are anxious to continue developing the forms that we prefer, that earned us recognition, and that, we hope, will bring us fame and great commissions. We then have to make some difficult decisions. Either we limit our work to the building types and regions for which our style is well suited, or we modify the forms that gained us success to respond with honesty to the varied requirements of today's projects. Both of these approaches are healthy and recognize the potential conflicts between our quest for form and our responsibilities. Both require a personal discipline. Deciding between doing what we know will be well accepted because it is "correct" and doing what we believe is "right" becomes wrenching when we decide to accept the full range of contemporary projects but still want to continue using and refining and consistently imposing on these projects our preferred set of forms.

Accepting the full range of projects of our time is not necessarily a strategy for professional success because it carries too many burdens. It comes from the urge to be a complete architect who responds to all the needs our world presents us. It is based on the belief that the architect's place is on the front lines, not in an ivory tower. To consistently make high art from the front is difficult, probably impossible, but an architect can always do good work, and when a designer manages to make a building into a work of art, under these circumstances, the internal satisfaction is incomparable.

The architectural culture pressures us to design with the correct forms and attitudes. When we are young these pressures are hard to resist because they seem natural to us. We have the example of most of the very talented architects of today who work with the consistent formal system of a school or a personal signature. By talented, I mean those architects with the ability to design buildings with beautiful forms and spaces that engage and move us. They are the very same architects whose work I enjoy and respect. But when their attitude is emulated by architects of varying talents, it has a noticeably bad effect on our cities and on architecture. An important measure of the worth of an architect's work is its value as a model for others.

Ideologies

Any long-lasting intellectual or artistic pursuit requires an ideology, a framework of principles and ideas that explains and justifies our actions and gives them direction. An artist today needs a personal ideology in order to accomplish original work. We build our ideology using pieces we gather throughout our lives from parents, teachers, books, friends, other artists, and, most important, from our own thoughts and experience. We begin our careers supported mainly by an adopted framework, and throughout our lives we replace borrowed pieces with new ones that are more appropriate to ourselves. Because we share many sources, our personal ideologies have much in common with those of other architects of our time. If this were not so, we would not understand one another's architecture. In order to do significant work, however, we need to reinterpret and modify shared ideas and make them part of a personal body of thoughts. The more we develop our individual position, the more we move away from that of our peers. We must then keep in mind that only a very thin line separates originality from irrelevancy.

Personal ideologies and individual styles may be related and one might guide the other, but today they appear to be disconnected. Following personal beliefs may lead to inconsistency of forms, and trying to be stylistically consistent, under all circumstances, may lead to conflict with principles or responsibilities.

I speak of a personal ideology because ideology also means a prescribed body of ideas with a common purpose (for example, Communist ideology), which may be called a directed ideology. When we accept someone else's ideas as our own we in fact decline responsibility for our own life or work and forfeit our internal growth. Some leaders of modernism hoped that their ideas would be seen as so profound that they would guide every architect of our time. Fortunately for us, no one of them went very far, and most of their ideas are now in retreat. Le Corbusier probably came closest to realizing this dream; he was able to attract a large number of influential followers, and his thoughts continue to affect many architects. But although we continue to learn from his art, his ideas are now widely questioned or ignored. The lasting value of modernism is due, in part, to its having avoided becoming a directed ideology. It has remained an approach to architecture based on several shared insights and principles. It can thus grow and accommodate under its umbrella many quite different personal ideologies.

Clear principles and ideas organized into a personal ideology can give direction to our work and our careers. More important, they are essential in giving form and purpose to our lives. And our lives are the whole of which being an architect is only a part, although for some it can be the most important part.

A social compact

Our actions as architects can be measured by society, and, if they are found wanting, society can seek redress. Depending on the nature of the failing, we can be tried in civil or criminal courts and be found financially liable, lose registration, or spend years in jail. This is another characteristic unique to the practice of architecture. Legal exposure and accountability are practically nonexistent in the practice of other arts. These practical considerations affect our professional behavior, but our art is more deeply affected by how we judge our own actions.

We have a compact with society based on the correspondence between our understanding of our role as architects and what others expect of our actions. The health of our profession depends on the reliability of the compact. It establishes that society will respect us as professionals and artists and that we will perform our work in a responsible manner, maintaining high standards and caring for the public good. Architects are members of a well-defined group. What we do, and how we do it, reflects on us individually and also on the profession as a whole, establishing the level of trust and respect that architects are accorded.

The dictionary tells us that a professional is a person who publicly declares a commitment to behave in an exemplary manner according to the ethics and ideals of a select group that performs public services. Architecture is also a vocation. A "vocation" originally referred to a calling from God, and this idea still colors its present meaning of an individual commitment to undertake the obligations and perform the duties of a particular task or function in life with dedication. Declarations and dedications serve valuable purposes. They reassure society of our worth and dependability and give direction to our commitment.

Individual responsibility

For a society, the morality that matters is what guides our everyday activities. We praise those who go beyond what is expected of them, and we may show our collective gratitude by elevating them to the pedestals of heroes or saints. Our social health, however, depends on being able to trust our fellow citizens, especially those in whose hands we place major responsibilities, such as public officers, doctors, lawyers, and also architects. Society has a right to depend on our sense of responsibility and to expect that we will perform our duties well and will avoid actions that may adversely affect others. Society should also be able to expect that each new building will enrich people's lives; that each one of us will contribute, to the best of our abilities, toward making our cities more livable, beautiful, and exciting.

In the early years of my career, my goals were those of all young architects with some talent: to design good buildings, see them built, and have my architecture accepted and admired by my peers. The goals of acceptance and admiration partly conflict with each other. A design has better chances of being accepted if it conforms to the consensus of the profession. To be admired, a design needs to break new ground, diverging somehow from the consensus. The natural reaction in our youth, and the safest course in those circumstances, is to try to create designs that conform to the architectural trends we most esteem, exemplifying an important idea or refining an accepted formal approach. We may also try to develop a newer and more daring version of the formal systems

107. *Cesar Pelli at Gruen Associates, City Hall, San Bernardino, California, 1972*

used by architects we respect. In our early years, we experiment with many options until we find the approach that best suits our ideals, our talents, and our opportunities.

I designed the San Bernardino City Hall (fig. 107) shortly after joining Gruen Associates. It is one of the most theoretically correct of my designs. It expresses my view of the nature of today's buildings in a transparent, almost didactic manner. Its structure and function and its internal orientation in response to the desert climate are clearly resolved. It was one of the first buildings ever to define its complex three-dimensional volume by a taut two-dimensional glass surface. When I visited it after it was completed, I was delighted with the result. The building also received considerable acclaim from the architectural culture. However, after my first pleased reactions to the success of the building and my artistic intentions, I started sensing that all was not right. No one ever criticized the design, except for myself. I could see that the building I designed was not helping its urban surroundings, was not making the city center better by its presence. The abstract nature of the design connected the building with current architectural preoccupations but disconnected it from something more important, its place. The design belonged to me and to the architectural culture, but it did not belong to the city of San Bernardino. Experiencing the rift between theory and reality in my own design was disturbing. I started to reconsider many beliefs that I had until then embraced. Perhaps only when we confront our inner conflicts do we get to truly know ourselves. I continued searching for clarity and excitement in my designs, but I began to try to make them appropriate to site and purpose.

In 1981, my firm was being considered for the design of a new building for the Graduate School of Administration (Herring Hall) at Rice University. Rice has a beautiful campus. It was planned in 1908 by Ralph Adams Cram, who also designed its first buildings and set the tone for future ones (fig. 108). The buildings are architecturally "incorrect." They do not respond to any clear historical or local tradition, or to their construction technology. However, they respond well to their purpose and to the Houston climate, and they create a most successful place. They have always been enjoyed by students, faculty, and alumni, who disliked the "modern" buildings built at Rice in the 1960s and 1970s. This issue arose during our selection interview with the building committee of the university's board of trustees. I was asked if I could design a new building compatible with those designed by Cram. I replied that I was in sympathy with these goals and that, if selected, I would do my best to meet them. But I could not promise that I would achieve those objectives because I would not design a building that lacked

authenticity in its expression of contemporary culture and technology. What was natural for Cram in the early twentieth century would be false for me more than seventy-five years later.

To my surprise, we were awarded the commission, and I embarked on a period of introspection, first to ascertain, given the conflict of values, what was most important. With thought, the answer became clear: the unity of character and scale of the campus had to come first. My responsibility to the place and the users was greater than an allegiance to a system of forms. However, I did not want my design to be banal or false. I then had to consider, in this new light, what makes a design authentic. I reasoned that integrity in architecture rests primarily on the honest and intelligent expression of its place, purpose, and time. Expression of place and purpose are easy to understand, but to be true to our

108. Ralph Adams Cram, Fondren Hall, Rice University, Houston, Texas, 1912 time is an unclear proposition. Our time is witness to many conflicting aesthetic and intellectual preferences. I was seeking an objective way to link my design with our time. I knew I could avoid elements such as classical capitals or arches with keystones, which are strongly associated with architectural styles of other times. This is almost an axiom for modern architects. It slowly became clear to me that I could also reinterpret modernism's respect for structural expression and try to make evident the nature of the very economical construction system used at Rice University. It occurred to me that construction systems offer us the least capricious connection with our time because those that are not of our time are either unavailable or unaffordable. This approach allowed me to design a building that belongs to the family of forms of Rice University and that also, although it does not look like an International Style building, is clearly modern.

The only construction system that satisfied Rice's budget and design guidelines was brick veneer on metal studs, supported by a lightweight steel frame. All recent buildings for the campus were built in this manner, although they were made to look like load-bearing brick masonry. Our design for Herring Hall unfolded as an exploration of the artistic possibilities of brick-veneer construction and of ways of expressing its nature with clarity. This was a new concept. The substance and appearance of Herring Hall (fig. 109) are unlike those of the buildings designed by Cram; it is a structure of our time. However, it connects with the architecture of the Rice campus in its typology, massing, materials, colors, and the density and rhythm of its detailing. It has been received by the university community as a fitting new member of the Rice family of buildings.

The experiences of the San Bernardino City Hall and Herring Hall provided me with new intellectual tools with which to respond to similar problems. They were also critical in helping me to better understand myself and my responsibilities. Most projects bring opportunities for theoretical exploration. Sometimes they also present us with inner conflicts. We can ignore them and keep on doing what we have learned to do well, or we can take them as opportunities to challenge ourselves and our beliefs.

*Opposite
109. Cesar Pelli &
Associates, Herring
Hall, Rice University,
Houston, Texas, 1984*

CONCLUSIONS

The many connections of architecture with the world limit our design, but also give it great strength. These roots nourish us and make architecture a very sturdy art. The better we understand them, the more pleasure we can derive from our work and the easier it is to respond to the diverse circumstances of our design. All connections affect architecture. Time, construction, place, and purpose do so primarily through our buildings. Culture, design process, constituency, and our principles affect us directly.

The art and practice of architecture are immensely rich and complex. The eight connections I have discussed provide good vantage points from which to observe critical aspects of architecture. Each connection allows us to focus our attention on a particular set of issues affecting our art today. Despite the diversity of its connections, architecture is a single entity. It is the nature and health of its totality about which we care. Observations and ruminations have led me to a number of conclusions, and these appear throughout this book. Following are the most salient ones, especially those that reveal weaknesses in today's architecture. I hope we might be able to correct them.

Modernity is our inevitable condition. Great and irreversible changes in our construction systems, in the purpose of our buildings, in our own culture, and in our constituency have defined for us a new time, *our time*. This period is of one piece. It first began to affect architecture in the mid-nineteenth century and continues today. *Modern architecture* is the architecture of *our time*. It includes the work of all architects who sought a new architecture, starting with Paxton's Crystal Palace. This inclusive modernism left us a rich legacy of valuable models and approaches. International modernism, a key episode in this movement, gave us many theories, some useful, such as the social role of architecture, and some of questionable value, such as adherence to a narrow formal system. Today, they all should be reconsidered.

The dominant construction system of our time is *frame and enclosure,* which replaced *load-bearing stone.* The changed nature of construction provoked and became the main justification for a new and modern architecture. It is still the most objective way to connect our buildings with our time, free from passing styles and fashions. New construction technology has increased our design possibilities, but it is more remote and abstract than earlier ones based on crafts. Each architect has to make a special effort to understand the nature of today's construction for the design to reflect it with integrity.

The parts owe deference to the whole. Thus we judge our architectural education not by itself but in relation to our whole career, and we judge our careers in relation to our whole life. We should also judge our buildings not by themselves but in relation to their urban context.

Cities are our most important responsibility. They are the test of our ideas. The conceit that a city can be designed, just like a building, has done much harm. Also harmful are the fashion for highly distinctive personal styles and the general disregard for city character and traditional contexts. Making a building one with its place has been a constant goal of architecture throughout the ages. Technological and cultural changes have weakened this critical relationship, and it is the responsibility of each one of us today to bring it back into our work.

The rules that our profession uses today to define what is desirable in architecture put too much emphasis on originality. The state of our cities and the quality of the main body of our buildings indicate that these rules are unsound and need to be corrected.

In shaping and trying to advance our art, we seek models that can serve us as guides. Painting has been an important model for us in this century. We have learned a great deal from it and have been energized by its achievements. However, we also accepted some notions that suit painting well but are harmful to architecture. The need to weed the unhealthy from the healthy lessons is now overdue. For example, we should reconsider ideals such as artistic freedom and aesthetic consistency. They may not suit our needs. Regaining the balance of our relationship with other visual arts has acquired urgency as we enter a new era of artistic collaborations.

Design is the craft an architect needs to master. We create our art through it, and it is the source of our daily pleasures and irritations. Our understanding of the design process is thickly overlaid with romantic images and myths. They often get in the way of our work and enjoyment. We should look dispassionately at how we do what we do and reserve our fire for our designs. We might then accept that architecture requires collaboration, that a well-structured process benefits the building and the art, and that our practices also need to be designed.

We architects work for others, as painters used to do. We must produce what is needed of us and, if we can, make it art. This is not a weakness in our discipline but a source of strength. We respond to the requests of our clients, to the needs of users of the building, to the media that will diffuse our work, and, most important, to society—the ultimate recipient of all buildings. It seems only right to put public concerns ahead of private ones, to accept that the public aspects of buildings, such as their facade or silhouette, should take precedence over private ones, such as their functional or structural clarity.

The design of buildings is entrusted to us, the architects. All issues of art and responsibility, efficiency and ethics depend on us. We need a firm intellectual backbone, deeply felt ideals, and a moral compass to act honorably, because the contemporary world has placed many temptations and pitfalls in our path. Our actions affect our work, our constituency, and our profession. We owe it to them and to ourselves to do our very best, every time.

PHOTOGRAPHY CREDITS